Creative
Worship

Services from Advent to Pentecost

Creative Worship

Written & Edited by Ian Price & Carolyn Kitto

WOOD LAKE BOOKS INC.

CREATIVE WORSHIP was first published in Australia with the title NEW DAWN, by MediaCom Education Inc.

Wood Lake Books editor: Mike Schwartzentruber
Cover design: Margaret Kyle
Cover art: Barbara Houston

Wood Lake Books acknowledges the financial support of the Government of Canada through the Book Publishing Industry Development Program (BPIDP) for our publishing activities.

At Wood Lake Books, we practice what we publish, being guided by a concern for fairness, justice, and equal opportunity in all our relationships with employees and customers. We recycle and reuse and encourage our readers to do the same. Resources are printed on recycled paper and more environmentally friendly groundwood papers (newsprint) whenever possible. The trees used are replaced through donations to the Scoutrees for Canada program. A portion of all profits is donated to charitable organizations.

Permissions
Scripture quotations are from the New Revised Standard Version of the Bible *(except where otherwise indicated or copyright sought and granted)* copyright 1989 by the Division of Christian Education of the National Council of the Churches of Christ in the USA.
Used by permission. All rights reserved.
Paraphrases by Ian T. Price

Canadian Cataloguing in Publication Data
Price, Ian, 1953-
  Creative Worship
Includes bibliographical references.
ISBN 1-55145-461-0

  1. Public worship. 2. Worship (Religous education) I. Kitto, Carolyn. II Title
BV25.P74 2002   264   C2001-911640-3

Published by Wood Lake Books Inc.
9025 Jim Bailey Road
Kelowna, British Columbia, Canada V4V 1R2
WEB: www.joinhands.com

Printing 10 9 8 7 6 5 4 3 2 1

Printed in Canada

Creative Worship

Contents

Where morning dawns and evening fades
you call forth songs of joy.
Psalm 65:8 NIV

Introduction

T. S. Eliot wrote that at the still point of the turning world, "there is neither from nor toward…neither arrest nor movement," only a "white light still and unmoving."[1]

Life is lived apace. The fury of a thousand demands robs our souls of spirit. Where can we find that place of connection – connection with God, with one another, and of course, with our very self?

This is a book about worship. It offers liturgies for some of the church's great celebrations. It is a simple attempt to help those who are looking for some stillness, as we move through the great festivals of the faith and find a "white light still and unmoving."

It is a time for us to remember that the God who created is that "still point of the turning world." The God of the ages, creator, liberator, incarnate presence, redeemer, and sustaining Spirit, is with us. What might God want of us? What new things are waiting to be born among us?

We celebrate all that God in Christ has meant to us. We look forward to what is yet to be.

These liturgies take us from Advent to Pentecost. They seek to tell the story of faith. You will find services for Christmas. A Service of Solace remembers with love and thanksgiving those who have died. We will worship together at New Year, as we witness a new year dawn.

We will journey with Jesus through the last hours of his life, with a Passover re-enactment, a Tenebrae service, a Good Friday liturgy focused on Christ's "seven words from the cross," and we will cry "Alleluia" in joy on Easter morning. For Pentecost there is an Agape meal for use in homes or at church, including a celebration of gifts and graces.

For each there is a full liturgy. We have sought out poems, readings, songs, and ideas to provide a full worship experience. However, our hope goes far beyond this. We hope these will be a beginning point – a place to shape the best each individual congregation can offer to God in worship. We pray that when people come to churches to worship, perhaps for the first time in many years, they will find communities so alive in God that they will experience the fullness of God.

Choose songs and hymns that work best in your congregation. Let the prayers be from the heart of your people. Let this be a time of celebration. Everything in this resource is intended to be an example only. Make it live!

There are many people who have contributed to these services and the ideas behind them. There are the named contributors, all of whom are gifted and caring people. But there are many more.

There are congregations in Goodwood, Noarlunga Centre, and Highgate, South Australia, who endured, laughed, and cried their way through years of liturgical highs and lows. There are teachers, seminar leaders, and house churches who have brought unique insights and spirit to life's journey. There are musicians, poets, preachers, prayers and singers, children, youth and adults, all with gifts and graces that have brought worship to life.

So rich is the tapestry of the community of God's people, that in a sense no one can be said to write anything when it comes to liturgy. It swells up from deep inside the tradition that is the church. It is our living language as we merge with God in a song of unparalleled joy, pain, and celebration.

In this resource, you will find words. Some will please – some will dismay. Some will represent great hymns of the scripture and the church, some will be incidental. Our singular hope is that you will take them and use them. Shape them, so that the voice behind them is unmistakably that of your community. We have provided the words on disc, so that you can rework them for your own purpose.

Where material has come from another source, every care has been taken to source permission for its use, and of course this cannot be changed. All else, however, is offered only as a suggestion and may be modified for use in congregations. Choose the music that will work well for you. Add prayers, puppet scripts, and drama.

Sometimes we have included music for parts of the service. This is the case where we have discovered that something worked particularly well. The songs, hymns, and carols are all suggestions only. They are included to make life a little bit easier.

With regard to poetry, drama, or contemporary readings, they are the work of the authors unless otherwise indicated. Permission is given to make copies for use in a service of worship. All other copyrights are reserved. With regard to material from other sources, normal copyright requirements hold. We have sought permission to print that material for this resource only.

Have fun with your worship, and may the living Spirit of God enthuse all that we do together.

Ian Price

Chapter one

Worship for All

The dawn of a new era has arrived with the new millennium. Futurologists and social researchers have been busily writing books and making predictions about the millennium for more than a decade. Sometimes one wonders if they are predicting the future through observing and analysing trends, or shaping the future by convincing us to behave in certain ways.

Amongst the predictions they make is one of a religious revival. Naisbitt and Aburdene devote a whole section of their book *Megatrends 2000* to this religious revival. The figures they quote leave no doubt that, world-wide, there is growing religious practice. Religious belief, whether fundamentalist, traditional or mystical, is intensifying as a way of contending with rapid change and an uncertain future. There are expectations that a new millennium might just offer a new start – or perhaps even new chaos or calamity. Christians can affirm that God is at work in the midst of all this. We are invited to join God in the creation of new possibilities and dimensions of life.

In moments of uncertainty and unpredictability, people seek religious expression and experiences. Together with heightened expectations and hopes for a new beginning, we will also seek a sense of community. At Christmas, New Year, and Easter, people come to worship looking for meaning and hope. People come to worship at times of special significance or celebration. People come seeking to give spiritual expression to the changes that they are experiencing and the hopes they have for the future.

There are at least three important questions for our congregations.
> What will people be looking for when they come?
> What will they discover when they come?
> How will we connect with each other?

The ways in which we respond to these questions will prove important in connecting with those who come. Our goal is to provide worship that engages the lives of those attending, to present the gospel in helpful and creative ways. This window of opportunity to connect with people's lives and searches is uniquely offered by this moment of history and by God.

Feasts, celebrations, and festivals
Have you noticed that we now have celebrations for Christmas in July? Have you ever wondered why? Philip Clark (radio announcer with the ABC in Sydney) asked Hugh Mackay (sociologist and social commentator) "Why?"

I think what we are looking at is a yearning in this community to have more festivals – more celebrations as a means of making us feel more confident in our identity and as a means of reassuring us that the community is really functioning.

Finally, people are saying we are tribal creatures. The herd instinct is very strong. We don't have enough togetherness, we don't have enough communal activity…the surge in interest in ANZAC day and Christmas in July is a symptom of a community looking for signs that it is a community.

I think all this is a really healthy sign that we are beginning to realise we don't spend enough time together. We don't have enough formal feasts, celebrations and festivals of various kinds.

These formal feasts, celebrations, and festivals are the formal feasts, celebrations, and festivals of the community and they can be the formal feasts, celebrations, and festivals of the church and the community. The church can respond to this yearning by inviting the community to be a part of its celebrations and festivals. In *Creative Worship* you will discover some of the feasts, celebrations, and festivals of the church which can also have value in the community and which can be community celebrations. They have all been developed with the community in mind.

Beyond the party
This yearning is deeper than simply wanting to "party." It has spiritual expression and explorations as well.

People are seeking inspiration

People are looking for something that motivates them for life, just as a writer or artist waits for their inspiration before taking the next step in producing their masterpiece. Such inspiration often comes from the helpful truths that Christians have always known. We do not need to strive to be profound or complicated. People are drawn to the story and life of Jesus and they identify with the gospel. The best sermon will be simple and helpful. Our message will make some sense out of ordinary, everyday life. The inspiration people will be seeking will involve a spiritual influence to be experienced – an experience of God.

People are seeking inclusion

It is a sense of inclusion which values who I am as a unique person. My uniqueness will be honored and connected with others. As well as engaging together in worship we will share stories which reflect our mutual humanity and the ways each of us makes sense of life. Too often the church has developed a sense of "them" and "us" – people seek "we."

People are seeking identification

> People are looking to see something of who they are – their needs, their hurts, their hopes and their joys – reflected in the worship and the gathered community. This grows the confidence that the community is working and will work for and with them. Together we affirm that we have a role to play in the unfolding mystery of life in which God is vitally interested.

God works through the ways in which people are seeking. God honours the search and blesses the searcher. Paul's advice to the church on how to relate to the community was

> Conduct yourselves wisely toward outsiders, making the most of
> the time. Let your speech always be gracious, seasoned with salt,
> so that you may know how you ought to answer everyone.
> *(Colossians 4:5, 6)*

God is not far from each one of us

The task of the Christian church in our time is crystallized in Paul's great sermon, preached to the Greeks on Mars Hill in Acts 17. Paul meets people where they are at, on their terms. These three steps from Paul offer us a helpful process for today.

First, he honors their search and affirms it. He recognizes that they are religious people (verse 22). The symbols of religious searching today are obvious when we take the time to look. Although not immediately recognizable in organized Christianity as symbols of faith or as struggles with faith, they are there, unique in each context.

Second, Paul uses their own religious symbols (an idol with the inscription "To an unknown god") as a beginning point for talking about God (verse 23). Our cultures offer multitudes of beginning points for talking about God. As one example – the rise in interest in science fiction, television shows such as the *X-Files* and *Star Trek* and movies such as *The Matrix* and *Star Wars* have at their heart profound religious questions. The movie theatres have become the pulpits of our time and offer images and stories that can be beginning points for talking about God.

Third, Paul quotes one of their own poets (verse 28) to share about Jesus. Perhaps the poets of our time are the songwriters and singers lamenting and celebrating life. Many secular songs offer the words to share about Jesus. Using the rhythm and style that people are used to and with which they are most comfortable, helps them to relax and opens them to listening.

As we share feasts, celebrations, and festivals together, the most awesome thing is that "God is not far from each one of us – we are all (God's) offspring." *(Acts 17:27,28, paraphrase)*

Chapter two

Come, Lord, Come

Advent

The season of Advent begins the Christian year. The word advent comes from two Latin words, *ad* and *vene,* meaning "come to." In the four weeks of Advent, we celebrate the God who comes.

We celebrate God's coming to liberate. We remember those who waited for the coming of the Messiah, focusing on the hope and longing for salvation that beat within the heart of the Hebrew people. We express our faith that in Christ that hope has been fulfilled, the waiting is done. Now the acceptable time of the Lord has come. We sing God's praise with Mary. Our hearts blaze with the passion of the Baptist. We weep gentle tears with Zechariah, Simeon, and Anna at the fulfillment of the dream, and lift our voices in awe:

> *Now let your servant depart in peace according to your word,*
> *for my eyes have seen your salvation.* (Luke 2:29, paraphrase)

We also celebrate the God who comes to us. Each of us has a story – unique, powerful, and beautiful. The wonder of faith is that God comes to us in grace, comes even to *me!* Our God is an intimate, personal being who dwells within. The Holy Spirit comes to us, renewing, refining, affirming, directing and empowering. It is good news! God comes, not as an alien, hostile, blaming judge, but as a loving, saving, longing friend. We worship the God who comes to us now.

Yet there is more. There is a future dimension. Advent lifts up the God who came in Christ. It celebrates the saviour who comes, even now, to each and every soul. And it points to a future coming. The faith of the church is that Christ will come again. Advent affirms that whatever the future holds, God holds that future. For individuals it is the belief that death has no sting (1 Corinthians 15:55), that we have an inheritance which is eternal life.

Advent also affirms that if life were to come to an end, God would have yet another thing in store. The apocalyptic message (often strange to contemporary ears) has at its foundation the faith that whatever happens, God will triumph. In an age of population explosion, ecological uncertainty, and the awareness that science cannot solve all problems, this is an emerging and important belief. When there is nothing, there is God!

So, at the beginning of the Christian year, we have a season that acts as a kind of overview of faith. We look back to see what God has done. We look within to see what God is doing. We look ahead to acknowledge what is yet to be – the advent of our God, the coming again of the Creator, Redeemer, and Sustainer.

What is the spirit of our Advent worship?

First, there will be a sense of movement. We begin with a sense of wonder, uncertainty, and waiting. At first, we are not sure that we can trust what we are perceiving. Can this be true? Is this the hour? Has all we have dreamed of finally become a reality? We are waiting, waiting, waiting. We know this sense of careful preparation and expectation, for it is carried in many communities by the preparations for Christmas. In the wide eyes of children, agog at the tinsel and toys that fill our shops, we see one expression of the spirit of the season of Advent.

It cannot stay there, however! It must move to the humility and obedience of Mary, Joseph, and the others to whom messengers brought words that are both exhilarating and terrifying. We are overwhelmed with awe that God should be concerned with mere mortals. Our soul "magnifies the Lord," for "the Mighty One has done great things for me." (Luke 1:46–49) There is a sense of submission to the very will of God – a willingness to be drawn into the drama of salvation.

This is no insipid tale. Advent is also a time of harsh and challenging words. In John the Baptist, we find a prophet who drives home to us the cost of faith. God is a jealous God, who demands much of us. If we are to be a community of faith, God's own children, then there is a cost, and we must be prepared to be sharers in the redemption that is won at such a deadly price.

Ultimately, the movement that begins in waiting ends in an exclamation – God triumphs over all that would distort, dehumanize, and debase. This is our Advent faith.

The service of worship that follows could be used at the beginning of Advent or as a special celebration. It draws on the three aspects of Advent described above.

For this service, you will need:
- a traditional Advent wreath (three purple candles, a blue candle for week three, and a central white candle – the Christ candle) placed on the communion table
- worship leaders to lead the liturgy and prayers, and to light the candles
- readers
- a person to play Zechariah
- a soloist for the *Magnificat*
- a preacher.

THE GOD WHO COMES

Welcome and greeting

Leader: The abiding love of the God of the Ages be with you.
People: *And also with you.*

Leader: Let us greet one another in grace.
People: *The peace of God be always with you.*

(People are invited to exchange the peace with *the words:*
The peace of God be always with you.)

Leader: Let us worship the living God!

Waiting for the Messiah

Leader: We light the first candle – the candle of Hope.
(The candle is lit.)
Out of the darkness there grows a glimmer,
out of the darkness there emerges a vision.
It is the dream of the exodus, the quest for shalom.
It is the possibility of redemption,
and the realization that God is at work.

Song Light One Candle for Hope

Reading Luke 1:5, 8–20

Prayer of adoration and praise

God of eternity, creator of all that is, we worship and adore you, for you give life to all living creatures and provide all that is necessary to sustain life. You come gently to us, breathing into us your gifts of grace, reminding us that we belong to you. Your radiance pierces our darkness, so that we see clearly who we are and what we might become. You affirm our goodness and invite us to be sharers in the joy of your realm.

Receive our praise, O God, for in you we find perfect beauty, absolute justice, and eternal mercy. Through Christ our Lord we pray. Amen.

Zechariah's Dream   *(see page 19)*

Song   O come, O come, Emmanuel

Leader: We light the second candle – the candle of Peace.
                (The candle is lit.)

                As in the days of the prophets, we cry, "Peace, peace," where there
                is no peace.

                We long for your kingdom to come fully in justice and love.
                We are waiting, Lord, waiting and watching.

                Come to us, we pray. Come as the dawn, radiant in splendid peace.
                Shine upon us with your saving grace.
                Bring us your peace.

Song   Light One Candle for Peace

Reading   Luke 1:39–49

Prayer of confession

                Why do we doubt you, all wise and knowing God? You wait patiently for us to join in the dance, but we are too busy with our own frantic steps. You speak to us quietly, whispering a love song of grace and salvation, but we cannot hear you through the din of our own amusement. You reach out to us to take your hand and tread the paths of peace and wholeness, but we are rushing headlong into oblivion, enticed by the illusion of power, wealth and fame.

                Forgive us our pride and foolishness, we pray. Help us to centre our being in you, that we may put aside our pretences and live in the freedom of your Spirit. Deliver us, O God, from all that impedes our faith. Deliver us from ourselves and set us free. In the name of Christ we pray. Amen.

Music ministry
                The Magnificat[2]

Leader: Like Mary, we make our offering of praise – we present to God our
                gift of love for the world.

Offertory

Offertory prayer

All: We dedicate our lives to you, O God. With humble thanks we bring these gifts. Take us. Use us. Let us be your servants too. Amen.

Leader: We light the third candle – the Candle of Joy.
(the candle is lit)

God speaks, and hearts run apace, beating, pounding with excitement.

Could it be true? God with us – taking on our flesh, living our life, dreaming our dream?

"Look, the virgin shall conceive and bear a son, and they shall name him Emmanuel." (Matthew 1:23)

Song   *Light One Candle for Joy*

Reading   Matthew 3:1–6

Address

Song   *Christ Be Our Light*

Leader: We light the fourth candle – the candle of Love.
(The candle is lit.)
Who shall we turn to, or where shall we go?
Christ alone has the words of eternal life.
Speak to us, Lord. Speak a word of love.
Speak a word of salvation for all people.
Speak a word for a new day.

Song   *Light One Candle for Love*

Prayers for others
Merciful God,
You love us infinitely more than we could ever imagine. Hear us as we bring before you the cares and concerns of our troubled world.

We pray for all who are suffering this day – the oppressed, the hungry, the homeless, and the ill.
(Silent prayer)

Come in the power of your Spirit and the embrace of your people.

We pray for all who hold the means of power – governments and community leaders, the wealthy, all who understand the ways of peace, all who decide the issues of life and death.
(Silent prayer)
Come in the power of your Spirit and the service of your people.

We pray for your church and its witness in the world – for evangelists, preachers, and teachers; for pastoral carers and healers; for prophets and apostles. Let each of us exercise our gifts to your glory.
(Silent prayer)
Come in the power of your Spirit and the ministry of your people.
We pray for our world, your creation. We pray for a desire to care for nature. Help us to care for the land, that future generations may enjoy its bounty. We pray for unity among the nations, that your will might be done in every land, by every person.
(Silent prayer)
Come in the power of your Spirit, and the presence of your people.

Grant us here, this day, grace in all we are and do; compassion for all people; strength for the journey; awareness of your leading; and a vision of eternity.

In the name of Christ we pray. Amen.

Hymn: *Come, Thou Long Expected Jesus*

Blessing

Leader: Now let your servants depart in peace,
            for you have shown us your salvation,
            promised of old.

All: Send us into the world to be a light to the nations.
            Make us shine with your glory.
            Lead us in your ways.

Leader: In the name of God, the Creator;
            in the name of God, the Savior;
            in the name of God, the Sustainer;
            in the name of the God who comes.

All: Amen.

Zechariah's Dream

(A monologue for use at Advent)

Ahh, there they are again, Anna and Simeon. Almost every day they come here – they call them "the Quiet of the Land" – what a strange name! It fits though; they are almost always silent, just praying – such simple, faithful folk.

Every day they are here, praying for the Messiah to come – watching, waiting, hoping. Not as silent as I was though! Let me tell you – it was the strangest thing. I was here in the temple, offering incense to the Lord.

I remember thinking, it felt just like Isaiah when he was called by God – kind of eerie, hushed and holy.

The mind plays tricks I thought, but then, there he was, Gabriel! You know, the angel.

He told me so himself.

He said we would have a son, a prophet, like Elijah. A prophet! We haven't seen one of those for generations.

I began to wonder, could this be the time of his coming, the Christ I mean?

Then I began to laugh – only on the inside, and very respectably.

We are old and Elizabeth is barren, and I thought I must be demented for even entertaining such a notion.

So I said, right out loud, "And how will I know that this is so?"

It was not the smartest thing I'd ever said.

"I am Gabriel. I stand in the presence of God, and I have been sent to you to speak and to bring you this good news."[3]

Then, because I had been a bit cheeky not believing him, he struck me dumb, until the child was born.

Some "good news"!

So I waited. Just like them.

Waiting, watching, wondering.

Would he come?

And then what?

Would we have a king once more?

Would we be free?

I wonder.

FOUR LITURGIES FOR THE ADVENT WREATH

The lighting of the Advent wreath candles can be an excellent opportunity to invite new families to the church to participate in worship. Even very young children can participate by asking the question "Why do we light the *(first)* candle?" and so on.

The family members are invited to work out the best way to divide the readings between them. You may need to give them instructions in how to use microphones, where to stand, and when to light the candles. The liturgies are intended to be used as calls to worship.

Each Sunday, the candles from the previous week(s) are lit prior to the beginning of worship. The central Christ candle is lit Christmas Day.

The first Sunday of Advent

Leader 1: Sing to the Lord a new song;
sing to the Lord, all the earth.
Sing to the Lord, bless his name;
tell of his salvation from day to day.
Declare his glory among the nations,
his marvellous works among all the peoples.
(Psalm 96:1–3)

Leader 2: Why do we light the first candle?

Leader 3: The first candle is the candle of peace. It reminds us that God wants all people to live together in harmony. God has promised that the Holy Spirit will live forever in our hearts to bring peace.
(The first candle is lit.)

Leader 4: Let us pray.
God of peace and mercy, come to us now in the fullness of your Spirit, that we may know your peace and forgiveness. Help us to worship you, to hear your Word, and to respond with faithfulness. Help us to be like Jesus in all we are and do. Amen.

The second Sunday of Advent

Leader 1: Someone is crying out in the wilderness:
"Prepare the way of the Lord, make a straight path for him to travel." *(Matthew 3:3, paraphrased)*

Leader 2: Why do we light the second candle?

Leader 3: The first candle was the candle of peace. This is the candle of hope. It reminds us to follow the example of the prophets who waited with hope for the coming of the Savior.
(The second candle is lit.)

Leader 4: Let us pray.
Loving God, you reach out to all people in love and kindness. Teach us your ways of justice and peace. Help us to look for you in every situation, and to await eagerly the new things you are going to do in our lives. Amen.

The third Sunday of Advent

Leader 1: The wilderness and the dry land shall be glad, the desert will bloom and rejoice… the blind shall see and the deaf hear; those who are silent shall shout for joy. *(Isaiah 34:1, 5–6, paraphrased)*

Leader 2: Why do we light the third candle?

Leader 3: The first candle was the candle of peace. The second candle was the candle of hope. This is the candle of joy. It reminds us of the song of joy that Mary sang when she heard the news that she was to bear the Savior of the world.
(The third candle is lit.)

Leader 4: Let us pray.
We praise and adore you, almighty God. Heaven and earth are full of your glory. All creation sings your praise and we offer you all thanks for the gift of this new day. May we be filled with the joy of advent, and rejoice in worship together. Amen.

The fourth Sunday of Advent

Leader 1: Look now, see what the Lord is doing! A young woman conceives and bears a son. He is called Immanuel: God with us.
(*Isaiah 7:14, paraphrased*)

Leader 2: Why do we light the fourth candle?

Leader 3: The first candle was the candle of peace. The second candle the candle of hope. The third candle was the candle of joy. This is the candle of love. It reminds us that God loves the world so much, that Jesus was sent to be its Savior.
(*The fourth candle is lit.*)

Leader 4: Let us pray.
Loving God, in Jesus we have seen how much you love us. In him we see all that we can become. You are always with us, to guide and strengthen and lead us. Help us to live our lives with confidence, as we seek to do your will. In the name of Jesus we pray. Amen.

Chapter three

One of Us

Christmas

The season of Christmas is, at one and the same time, the easiest season for us to work with and yet one of the most difficult. It is an excellent opportunity for the church to make connections with the community. Almost all of the Christian symbols are found in the celebrations of the wider community. People are more open to attending worship, and many are looking for a family experience to express the joy of the season. Parents, who may have little to do with children's and youth programs, willingly attend nativity pageants and end-of-year celebrations. It offers us a bridge to the community.

Conversely, it is also one of the most difficult times for worship leaders. What is left to say about Christmas? For at least six weeks beforehand, we are overrun with the *junk* of Christmas. Long before we ever get near the beginning of the liturgical season, we have sung most of the carols, and every sweet and sickly way imaginable to present the Christmas story has been thrust in our faces.

Here is the great challenge for the liturgist and preacher. How do I present Christmas in a fresh and engaging way, at least partially free from the overlay of the culturally crass messages that inundate us?

There are a number of things that will help.

1. Focus on the community

It is as important to ask the question "Who will be present?" as it is to ask "What does God want us to say?" If we can grasp that this is a time for worshipping with the community, then we are halfway home. In the design of the various services of worship we will want to offer, it will be the whole community that we will have in the forefront of our minds.

What will make first-time worshippers have a sense of home? How can I make connections with their life stories? How can we connect the present reality with the greater reality of Christ and God's purpose for the world? When are the times that the community will most easily worship?

2. Work with the culture, not against it

It's a case of damned if you do and damned if you don't! Many a fine sermon has been wrecked on the rocks of attacking the abuses of Christmas. For those for whom this may be one of the few times for attending worship, the subliminal and subtle messages may be the loudest they will hear. This is a time for celebration not condemnation, community not separation, affirmation not rejection.

At the same time, if we are seen to be totally indistinct from the culture, why would anybody bother with us? The key is to do both things well and positively. We begin with connection points in the culture. We reinforce that we are a community together, avoiding anything that will convey an "us and them" mentality. We aim for some fresh and unexpected moments that will stop the participants in their tracks. This can be achieved in many ways – perhaps a short, punchy drama; perhaps a song that touches the heart; or maybe a sermon illustration that is one of those "aha" moments. In some way, we must move out of the comfort zones to offer a message that has the sense of exploring together a great truth, rather than a trite message or condemnation.

3. Strive for excellence

Excellence is expected today. Sloppiness is not tolerated. It may be the case that most people's primary experience of Christmas will be through the television. Televised carol services, world famous choirs, cathedral worship, and special variety shows abound in this season. Most of us do not have the resources or capacities to offer this level of expertise. Nonetheless, there are things we can do to ensure the things are done well and that we are thoroughly prepared.

- Ensure that those leading are properly **prepared**. This is a high season in the year, and poor readers, unrehearsed choirs and singers, and slapdash liturgy will be a barrier to worshippers' full participation. Many congregations have a rehearsal to ensure that the worship is worthy of God. This is especially important with inexperienced leaders. Gather together a team to prepare for the season's worship.

- **Highlight community**. The one thing that congregations have to offer that television cannot better is that sense of our community. Strive to grow a sense of belonging, ensuring that our language and attitudes are inclusive of all who are there. In one church, there was a person who was near the end of a long battle with cancer. It was to be her last Christmas. The minister brought in an easy-chair from the minister's vestry so that she could be there. It was a most striking symbol of the inclusiveness of the congregation and the desire for us all to be together. I doubt the family will ever forget that year. Nor will the congregation.

- Aim for **thematic consistency**. Much of what we do in the church is so familiar to us that we do not realize its complexity. The liturgical movements we take for granted are unknown to most people. Christmas is a time for keeping things simple. With the rush and hurry of this time, to keep things simple and smooth will allow people the space they need to worship.

- Be prepared to stick with just **one or two ideas**. It is tempting to try to tell the whole of the story in one hit, but we will only lose worshippers in the process. Settle for a single theme such as "Love for the least," or "Christ the center of Christmas," or "The babe born in each of our hearts." People will thank you more for inviting them to explore one or two ideas than if you overwhelm them with many.

- **Aim each year to do something stunning.** We may not have the best choir in town, but most of us can find a better than average soloist. Give everyone a beautiful flower to reflect upon during worship to convey the beauty, grace, and love of God. Have someone make a beautiful banner, or project an image, or design an audio-visual. Ask the congregation what gifts they have that could help. Even an outstanding floral display can do much to speak of the importance of what we are doing. Decorations can add much to the sense of festivity.

4. Remember the senses

Here is a special occasion when we can find different ways to communicate through the senses and the emotions. I very much doubt whether Christmas Eve or Christmas Day is the occasion for well-constructed teaching sermons, though I've endured a few over the years. Most of us want to laugh and cry together; to see and hear with delight; to touch, taste and smell the joyful presence of God coming through the season. In the forefront of our mind will be the question, "Have I provided a variety of ways for experiencing Christmas?"

5. Engage the children

In many places this will be an all-age experience. In many other places, children will be given lip service. This a time when children can easily be involved in leading the worship. They will know the carols – if we choose wisely. This is a time when stories can be used to convey the message. What a pity if the children's "bit" is confined to a "children's sermon"! This is also a time for appealing to the child in all us adults. Isn't that one of the keys to understanding the universal joy of Christmas? It allows us to be a little freer.

6. Be real about life

For many, Christmas will carry a fair burden of pain and unhappy memories. We will do well to honor these feelings and offer some hope and love.

7. The focus is God

Above all else, make God the focus. This is a time of worship, and we want to convey just how deeply we love God, how thankful we are for the birth of Jesus, and how much we long to serve our creator. Somehow we must convey a sense of adoration.

In the services that follow, you will find four liturgies for Christmas. The first is a Christmas Eve children's nativity. It is a simple retelling of the Christmas story. It is designed to involve children and engage their families. It might be used outdoors (weather permitting) in a car park or on a street side. The feel is of a community carol service.

The second service, *A Service of Solace*, is intended for those who would like to remember those loved ones who have died. It is especially relevant for the recently bereaved, but will also offer a moment of remembrance for many in the community. The first Christmas after a loss is tough. In communities where a congregation is engaged in conducting many funerals, this can provide a service to those we have served in this way.

The third service is a midnight communion service. As with the *Service of Solace*, there is an opportunity to light candles, so some facility to accommodate them will be important. This worship is intended to begin at about 11:15 p.m. with carol singing. The communion liturgy begins at midnight with the *Greeting*, so some attention to the allocation of time will be important. The aim is for a mixture of joy and sacredness. It is important to offer a breadth of experience rather than narrow the range of emotions. We are striving to convey the extraordinary gift that God is giving.

In a sense, Christmas morning virtually takes care of itself. The carols, the story, and the sense of the day itself will carry the liturgy. If attention is given to excellence and the ideas above, it will be a wonderful celebration. The feel of this service is of unbridled joy and simplicity. The worship is one act of adoration of God. In the worship below, a number of characters from history share what it means to be sharers in the incarnation. We are seeking to carry the idea that the birth of the Christ-child engages each of us, inviting us to welcome him into our lives.

STARRY NIGHT

A children's pageant

This service is intended as a family service for early evening on Christmas Eve. It will work best if it involves children from the Sunday school, kid's club, preschool or after-school care. Children who "turn up" can be given a costume if they want to participate. It is anticipated that children will lead most of the service. There are a number of places where children can lead the singing, including *O Christmas tree,* a version of Mary's song *The Magnificat*, *Donkey Donkey,* and the offertory carol *Silent Night.* There are also opportunities for children to participate in choral work, in the telling of the story, in poems and in the nativity play.

 The telling of the story begins with the decoration of a Christmas tree. The father or mother (your choice) is asked about the star and the tree, and takes up a book to tell the origins of Christmas. (The book should be a large Christmas storybook with the text of the script stuck into its pages.) As the story unfolds, children dressed as characters in the story make up the scene in the stable.

It is essentially a carol service that could be led outdoors in a public place like the parking lot of the church or on the tennis courts. It is intended to be a community time.

A stage or elevated area may be set up with a Christmas tree to one side. You will need a box of Christmas decorations, a rocking chair, and some Christmas presents under the tree. This is the area where the storyteller and children will decorate the tree. The central area can be set up with a stable-like structure at the back, with hay bales strategically placed for the children to sit on. This area becomes the scene for the nativity tableau that will develop through the reading of the story.

If you have a children's/youth band choir or orchestra that can accompany the carols, they may be situated on the side opposite the tree. This way they are part of the service and their contribution will be recognized by the congregation.

Some children will be included with the storyteller, helping to decorate the Christmas tree. You will need other children for the nativity dressed in traditional Christmas nativity garb. The principle characters are: Mary, Joseph, the innkeeper, angels, shepherds, and magi. Other children may fill roles as sheep, extra angels and crowd. The more the merrier! The goal is to create a sense of inclusive community.

If possible, the children will have prepared a Christmas card to give to the worshippers at the end of the service. For this service, you will need:
- a Christmas tree
- nativity
- costumes
- musicians
- singers
- worship leaders

STARRY NIGHT

Greeting and welcome

Carols   *The First Nowell*
While Shepherds Watched Their Flocks By Night (selected verses)

Prayer   Loving God, we thank you for this night, a night of excitement as we wait to celebrate again the birth of your Son. We thank you for the joyful sound of carols, the warmth of families together, the laughter of children, and the blessing of your presence among us.

May this worship remind us of your goodness to us. May we remember, with wonder, your gift of life, your gift of love, and the gift of yourself in Jesus.

For all you are to us, we give you our praise. In the name of Jesus Christ we pray. Amen.

Scripture   Matthew 1:18 – 2:6

Song   *O Christmas Tree*

(The storyteller and children involved in decorating the Christmas tree enter during the carol and proceed to decorate the tree. At the end of the carol they finish by placing a star on the top of the tree.)

Child 1:   Why do we put a star on top?

Storyteller: Because it reminds us of the star that led the wise men to Jesus.

Child 2:   Do you know a story that tells us about it?

Storyteller: Of course, it's Christmas and I have the story right here. Would you like me to read it to you?

Children: *(Excitedly)* Yes please!

(Storyteller sits in rocking chair with the book and the children sit around her/him.)

Storyteller: Once long, long ago, messengers of God said that one day God was going to send someone special into the world to build up God's kingdom.

The people waited and waited and sometimes wondered if God had forgotten. But God did not forget! God was waiting for just the right time.

Then one day, something wonderful happened. A baby called Jesus was born and during his life he showed everyone how much God loved them and wanted to be with them.

Carol *Infant Holy, Infant Lowly*

Storyteller: Do you know that before Jesus was born, God sent the angel Gabriel to a girl named Mary, who lived in the town of Nazareth? The angel told Mary that God had chosen her to give birth to a holy child who would be named Jesus. The angel then told her that this special child was to become great and would be known as the Emmanuel – God with us.

Mary was surprised and wondered "Why did God choose me?" But Mary wanted to do what God asked of her and so she said to the angel, "I will be glad to serve the Lord."
(Two angels enter to stand at the back near the stable as "Mary" sings.)

Solo *The Magnificat* (Choose a version such as *Tell Out My Soul.*)

Storyteller: Now after visiting Mary, the angel also appeared in a dream to Joseph, who Mary was going to marry. The angel told Joseph about the very special baby that Mary was going to have.

So Mary and Joseph were married and they lived together in the town of Nazareth.

A few months later, the Emperor Augustus decided to find out how many people lived in the country. Everybody was told to travel back to their home towns to be counted. So Mary and Joseph set out on a long journey to the town of Bethlehem where Joseph's family came from. Can anyone here tell me how Mary and Joseph traveled to Bethlehem?

Children: On a donkey.

Children's singing group *Donkey, Donkey*
>*(Mary and Joseph walk around the congregation. Children sing* Donkey, Donkey.*)*

Storyteller: The roads were pretty windy and rocky and sometimes they had to go up and down hills. They were getting very tired when, suddenly, they saw Bethlehem in the distance.
(Mary and Joseph stand outside the stable.)

Carol *O Little Town of Bethlehem* – omit verse 3

Storyteller: Who can tell me what happened when they first got to the town?

There was nowhere for them to stay. Bethlehem was crowded because a lot of other people had traveled there to be counted as well and all the inns were filled with people. Everywhere they went the owner would say, "Sorry, we're all filled." Or, "Sorry, there's no room here."

Mary and Joseph were getting a bit worried because Mary was about to have her baby and they wanted to find some shelter. *(The innkeeper enters from one side and Mary and Joseph approach her/him.)* At last a kind innkeeper said, "My rooms are all filled, but I have a stable you can use if you want to. The cattle are there and some cows and donkeys, but they won't bother you."

So off they went to the stable a little way out of the town.

That night the baby Jesus was born. There was no cot for Mary to put Jesus in so she wrapped him in strips of cloth and laid him in a manger. Who can tell me what a manger is? *(Get the children to respond.)*

A manger is where the food was usually placed for the animals to eat, but on this special night it was the perfect spot for Jesus to sleep in.
(Mary, Joseph and the innkeeper move into the manger.)

Carol *Away in a Manger*

Storyteller: While Mary and Joseph were still in the stable looking after Jesus, something very unusual happened out in the fields. The whole area suddenly filled with light and an angel appeared. The shepherds were frightened, but the angel said to them, "Don't be afraid, I have come to tell you some good news." The angel told the shepherds that a wonderful thing had happened. A baby had just been born in Bethlehem, a baby who had come to lead people to God. Then the angel told them where they could find Jesus. Suddenly, lots of angels appeared and they all began to sing and praise God for the birth of Jesus.

The shepherds decided to see if the angels were right and off they went looking for Jesus.
(The shepherds come to the manger with their sheep.)

Carol   *Hark the Herald Angels Sing*

Storyteller: Some time later, a bright star shone in the sky. There were some wise men from the east who studied the stars and they decided to follow it. And where do you think the star led them?

Children: To Jesus.

Storyteller: That's right, it led them all the way to Jesus.
(*The magi follow an angel carrying the star to the stable as the children sing. Youngest Sunday school children sing* Twinkle, Twinkle, Big Bright Star.)

Storyteller: When the wise men met Jesus, they knelt down and worshipped him and gave him gifts that were fit for a king. One gave him gold, another gave him frankincense, and another gave him myrrh.
(The kings come to the stable with their gifts.)

Carol   We Three Kings

Storyteller: So there we have it. (*Looking at the manger.*) That's the story of the first Christmas. All those people, not to mention a few angels, witnessed the birth of the Son of God – and we can witness it too.

Children: How?

Storyteller: Well, while it's true we can't actually be there, Christ is born in our hearts, you know. We experience the birth of Jesus in us, and know his love and presence too. Listen to this.
(*An older child reads the poem below.*)

Poem: One Child

One child, born for a multitude
One child, given just for me
One child, life of the world is he
One child, hope for us all.

Come Christ, shine in our darkness now
Come Lord, show us the way
Come Truth, freedom for all to bring
Come now, you are our way.

Lead on, gift of eternal life
Lead us, bringing us home
Lead Lord, liberty and truth to share
Lead Christ, you are our hope.

Carol   *O Come All Ye Faithful*

Christmas charity offering   (or other Christmas charity)
(Explain that the offering will be going to charity. It may be appropriate to describe one or two of the projects.)

Carol   *Silent Night (Sung as the offering is taken up.)*

Offertory prayer

Thank you, God, for all your gifts.
Thank you for hands to serve;
songs to sing;
love to share;
and gifts to give.
May these gifts we bring help those in need. Amen.

Prayer for others

Child one: Dear God, tonight we think of all the people who need your help.

Child two: We pray for people who are on their own.

Child three: Please give them a friend.

Child one: We remember all who are hungry.

Child two: Let there be enough food for all to share.

Child three: Let the hungry be fed, Lord.

Child one: We pray for all who have no home.

Child two:	May they find a place of shelter.
Child three:	Help the refugees of our world to find security.
Child one:	Dear God, remind your children that you came in Jesus to share your love with everyone.
Child two:	Make us generous in our care of others.
Child three:	May all the world know of your goodness and care.
Altogether:	Amen.

Carol   *Joy to the World*

(*During the singing of* Joy to the World, *the children hand out the Christmas cards they have made.*)

Blessing   This is the night on which the Christ was born.
May the joy of his coming be in our hearts.
May his love fill our souls.
May the hope of the gospel be in us forever.
May we share God's blessing with everyone we meet. Amen.

SERVICE OF SOLACE
A memorial service

The word solace has to do with providing comfort in a time of sorrow or trouble. For many of us, these words are so true at Christmas. As the streets are filled with the sound of songs of joy, and the world seems bent on creating an overwhelming sense of happiness, many are all too aware that they are living on the edge. The season is not for them. The pain of life wells up from within, and sadness fills the heart.

A *Service of Solace* at Christmas does two things. First, it offers time out. Where can one be with others without putting on the face of celebration? Where can one be with others in quietness to experience a kind of solitude within community? For the past several years our congregation has held this kind of service on Christmas Eve.

Some people will keep coming back year after year. Certainly it is to remember people they loved who are no longer there. Yet it is more. Folk share that they have discovered something healing and restoring in this time of worship. Here, there is permission to be quiet – to sit and reflect and take time out from the responsibilities and rush of life. It is a time of comfort for our inner being.

The second thing it does is offer a time for honoring our dead. Essentially, this is a memorial service. It recognizes that for many of us it is those who are absent that we wish most could be here. Most people, when asked about the best Christmases, will recount stories from their childhood family.

These memories are precious and as real today as ever. Our memories are a mixture of happiness and loss, of joy and pain. "I would love to have one more Christmas with Mum and Dad!" "Wouldn't it be great to be a family again?" For some adults, the loss is simply coping with the growing up of children, loosing that sense of the magic of Christmas.

There is a surprising power about this service. It touches the participants in profound ways, reaching deep into the soul and psyche. This has little to do with the liturgy or the preaching. The secret lies in providing space for us to explore our feelings. Lurking within are very powerful emotions, and our job is, with the utmost simplicity, to enable worshippers to live with them for a while.

The key is simplicity. In the preaching we want to do three things.

- Show that we understand this aspect of life. This is best done by story. This is not the occasion for dogma. It is all about compassion – passion with and for others.
- Share something of our own pain. We are exposing our common hurts. The preacher will enable this best by saying, "We all carry the hurts of life." Resist the temptation to "short circuit" the recognition of pain by moving from it too quickly. There is a right balance to be aimed for between not overdoing the pain and glib recognition.
- Offer a word of hope. The gospel declares clearly and strongly that God is with us in every aspect of life, and God is here now for us.

Many people come to this service with severe depths of depression. Consider having a counselor speak in addition to the preacher. This could be a Christian doctor, therapist, or social worker. This person can offer, ever so briefly, one or two simple ways to get through. Christmas is a critical time of the year for suicides, so having a professional offer some principles for coping is helpful.

This takes only five minutes and is not meant to be preachy. Over the years, the presentations have identified that grief is natural; it is always with us but we learn to bear it; and we are able to move on with it in meaningful and purposeful ways. To remind each other that we need one another's support will also help.

The **atmosphere** of this service is very important. It will have times of quietness and reflection. The key here is the music. The suggested hymns are chosen for their pleasant melody and familiarity. The voluntaries are soothing, and to have a soloist is helpful. The music, and in particular the soloist, will allow people time to express their emotions.

The climax to this service is the lighting of candles in memory of loved ones. A sand-filled tray such as a rectangular planter box could be used to hold the candles which people light. Some suitable decoration of purple cloth and flowers might add to the attractiveness of the display.

For this service, you will need:
- worship leaders
- preacher
- counselor
- candles and Christ candle
- a candle holder or tray with sand in it
- singing group/soloist
- welcomers

SERVICE OF SOLACE

Welcome

Call to worship

Leader: In the time of our sorrowing, God is there –

People: there in the embrace of loved ones –

Leader: there in words spoken with compassion –

People: there in the quiet places of the heart, in recalled, treasured memories.

Leader: Yes, God is there – and God is here.
Come, gracious God.
Come in quiet hope.
Come in gentle assurance.
Come in tender mercy.
Come with healing to make us whole.

Solo *Once You Had Silver*

Prayer O God of the ages, who from everlasting to everlasting grants us mercy, comfort, and hope, we turn to you this night to pause in the midst of all the celebrations to remember those we have loved who will not be with us.

We come seeking comfort for the pain of loss we bear. We remember with such fondness shared moments of joy, experiences that are lost to time but live forever in our hearts.

In truth, O God, we would like to have those times back again, to enjoy, however briefly, a conversation, an embrace, another occasion of joy and laughter. But they are gone, and we must content ourselves with memories of love and happiness.

Here, tonight, may we remember the good times. May we remember the special qualities of unique persons. May we celebrate life in all its goodness.

Grant us the healing of your Spirit's presence and the sure and certain knowledge of the gift of eternal life. In the name of the Christ we pray.
Amen.

Psalm 23

Carol   *Love Came Down at Christmas*

Reading   A Lament

> Where are you, God?
> Are you hiding?
> Has it become too difficult to show your face round here?
> There was a time when I would not have minded your absence;
> when I was young a different spirit beat within,
> and I was strong and needed less.
> Not so now – I really need you.
> I need someone to help carry these tired bones
> one more time around the block.
> I need someone to fashion words for all who ask me how I am,
> expecting faith and piety to flow.
> Yes there's a weariness upon me now,
> and I would like a day's rest –
> rest from this emptiness;
> and rest from this hollow ache;
> rest from uncertainty;
> and rest from my own questioning.
> Oh, it's okay, I know you're there.
> And all in all I know you care.
> It's just that it turned out differently, you know.
>
> So I will wait for you to come,
> and I will sing the song of faith,
> till love is born and life is whole again,
> and journey's end is won.

Carol   *Infant Holy*

Getting by, getting through, getting on   (A guest counselor)

Carol   *Silent Night*

Reading   Isaiah 40:1–5, 10–11

Reflection from ***Sing to the Lord a New Song***, by Susan Mangam, S.T.R.

New Life

Year after year in the springtime, I watch my neighbour's cows – watching for one who begins to withdraw from the herd and get that inward look. And when she doesn't show up at the barn for feeding time, I search the pastures and woods. I suppose it is part curiosity, part concern, and still a bit of human arrogance that assumes she won't make it without me (though only once in all these years did a cow need any help in giving birth). Most times I find the cow already crooning and licking over a little, wet, glistening white-faced creature. I've learned not to get too close; mama can be quite protective. For a few hours, mama and baby are alone. The calf is scrubbed and scrubbed. It stands, falls, stands, and learns which end of mama is full of milk. Then, side by side, they begin their first journey together. Ordinarily they stop as they near the herd, and mama steps back and presents her child. One by one, cows come to greet the newborn with a gentle sniff.

On a cold, rainy morning last spring, big old "Gramma" didn't show up at the barn. After a long, wet search, I found her way down in the woods with her newborn. I stopped a way off. Gramma looked at me, sang that low sweet sound, stepped back, and presented him to me. Never before had this happened to me – this sacred ritual of infinite courtesy. And after I, on my knees in the mud, had joyfully caressed the new life, and Gramma and he were heading to meet the others, I thought, "I'm a cow!" No. Gramma and I know differently. But I'm no longer an intruder: I am one with them!

Now it is dark winter, the time of gestation, when year after year we await the coming of new life. A young woman about to give birth and her husband seek hospitality and find it, not among human society, but in a cave with cattle. After the child is born and has a time of intimacy with his mother, he is presented in the animals' feeding trough. He is greeted by lowing sounds and warm breath from gentle muzzles. And as the invisible forces of the universe commune with the visible, those humans who are in harmony with Creation – the earth, sheep, plant life; the heavens, stars, planets, cosmic life – come to this cave singing praise and thanksgiving to the God of infinite courtesy.

(Printed in *Weavings*, November/December 1992. Used with permission.)

Song   The Turning Point of Time

Homily   (See page 37)

Prayer   Loving God, who in Christ has shown us how to live and the way of love, we would not pray only for ourselves, but think of all those who will this night carry the burden of loss.

We pray for all who will walk lonely hospital wards, anxiously watching and waiting with loved ones.

As dusk falls, we think of those who are alone, perhaps for the first time at Christmas.

We remember before you all who are estranged from family and friends, and bear the added burden of guilt or shame.

We pray for all who are suffering through illness, hostility, hunger, or homelessness.

Lord Jesus Christ, you came amongst us in simplicity. You lived among and for the poor and needy. You poured out your love upon all. Come amongst our need and misery this night. Grant the gentle touch of your presence to heal and relieve, to comfort and to strengthen. Come in the person of one of your followers. Come in the fullness of your Spirit, for we would know, in every land and every home, goodwill to all and peace among humankind. We pray it in the power of your holy name. Amen.

Memorial candles

Carols *Away in a Manger*
A Christmas Blessing

Blessing Deep peace of the running wave to you,
deep peace of the flowing air to you,
deep peace of the quiet earth to you,
deep peace of the shining stars to you,
deep peace of the gentle night to you,
moon and stars pour their healing light on you.
Deep peace of Christ the light of the world to you.
    (A traditional Celtic blessing)

Homily (An example)
A time for…

In the Old Testament book of Ecclesiates, there is a passage that has as its theme the idea that for everything there is a season, and a time for every purpose under heaven.

The book is the writing of a cynic, known only to us as "the teacher." It is part of an ancient collection of writings we describe as wisdom literature. The teacher is overwhelmed by the futility of life. What is the point of it all? All is vanity, a waste of time.

Like you, I have known my share of sadness. The deaths of those we love leave a certain emptiness, a void which defies comfort. In such times the teacher's words seem most apt. What is the point of life?

Life can seem hard enough, but for many, it is made all the harder when we try to resist the ebb and flow of all that comes our way. There is a futility to life, but it is the more so when we live life against the grain. The teacher is right when he says there is a time for birthing and a time for dying. Death is a part of life. There is a time to die, and a time to mourn, and a time to embrace life again.

As much as we might wish otherwise, we cannot control life. It has its times, and if we can learn from life, we will learn to be as fully present and accepting of this life as we can be. A modern trend has been to avoid the pain of death. Many people find it hard to be with a loved one at the point of death. Some refuse to ever see a person after death. Some refuse to allow their children to attend a funeral. It has been my practice to be as encouraging as possible to have children of any age be present at the point of death, and at funerals. It is not ghoulishness, but reverence that motivates me.

I remember at the time of my father's death we took our two young daughters to the viewing. It was a very precious and special time for us as a family. It was something we shared that brought us closer together. But it was also a telling moment, when one of them said, "He doesn't look like Grandpa, there's no life in him." We knew that Grandpa was gone, and we drew on our faith. We prayed and wept together, and later we celebrated all he was to us.

Death is one of the most important things that happen in our lives. For believers, it is the gateway to eternal life, the road to whatever wonders God has in store for us beyond the grave. What a pity to deny life by avoiding this most crucial moment. Is it any wonder that so many people are unprepared emotionally and especially spiritually for this, if they spend so much of their lives denying it?

It is so important that we be present and experience the fullness of life, including death.

If we can be present, we quickly learn that we need not fear. Fear of the unknown is one of the greatest fears of all. When we are present to the feelings and memories of the past, we learn the preciousness of life.

Jon Walton writes of an experience he had visiting the Edinburgh Festival Military Tattoo a little while ago.

There must have been a thousand bagpipers who marched away from us playing *Scotland the Brave*, and I swelled with pride because of my Scottish roots all mixed up with the Irish in me.

There in Edinburgh those thousand Scottish pipers finished *Scotland the Brave* and turned and marched back toward us from the far end of the esplanade. Now they marched and played at a slower pace, and I immediately recognised the tune they were droning, "Goin' home, goin' home, I am goin' home, Mommy's there spectin' me, Daddy's waiting too. Goin' home, goin' home, I am goin' home."

Tears started streaming down my face, poor sentimental sort that I am. And I realised that there is a home someplace that I do want to go back to, someplace where there is reunion and peace and joy, where the glow of human love meets the warmth of heavenly compassion."[4]

There is a time for being present, and a time for faith, and to live in this way makes possible a reunion of peace and joy, "where the glow of human love meets the warmth of heavenly compassion." Because of Christ, we have this assurance, that life does not end in death but lives on in the grace of God. We have a home. It is in the bosom of God's very self.

We celebrate the fullness of life, the fullness of faith, and the fullness of love.

In the death of those we love the best, we learn about life and death, and again the teacher of Ecclesiastes has something to say to us. "There is a time to keep, and a time to throw away."

I have had to learn to keep hold of those things that are life-generating, that create wholeness and goodness, and to simply let go of all the things I cannot change that will only leave me in deeper, unresolvable pain. We cannot change the things that happen to us, but we can choose our way of reacting. To seek for Christ in the midst of the pain, I have found, is the most precious thing. The comfort of the Lord is real and almost tangible.

Ultimately, the company of our life and our relationships are as important as anything we could ever achieve. In A. A. Milne's wonderful book *Winnie the Pooh*, there is this brief exchange.

Piglet sidles up to Pooh from behind.
"Pooh!" he whispers.
"Yes, Piglet?"
"Nothing," says Piglet, taking Pooh's paw. "I just wanted to be sure of you!"[5]

To experience true friendship in the midst of grief is everything. Someone once said, "True friends don't need to hold hands because they know the other hand will always be there."

Fullness of life, fullness of faith, fullness of love. "There is a time for every purpose under heaven."

What is this time? It is a time for remembering, a time for taking up those precious gifts that are the legacy of those who have gone before. It is a time for letting go, believing in the promises of God, who reached out to us in the birth of Jesus. It is a time for celebrating love, and knowing that in Christ, love lasts forever.

So let us enter a time of quiet reflection. We will be led in song as we prepare for prayer and an act of remembering. Let us thank God for life and love.

CLOTH FOR THE CRADLE
A Christmas Eve Eucharist

Christmas Eve is a wonderful time to worship. There is an air of expectation mixed with tiredness. We have been waiting, preparing, shopping for food and gifts, and now there is a sense of "All is prepared!" This celebration lends itself to candlelight, quietness, reflection, and contemplation. It is a time for being touched by the mystery of the faith – God is born among us. God dwells with us. God is present forever.

Christmas Eve can also be a time of some sadness. We cannot worship at Christmas without some sense of those who may not be present. Whereas the atmosphere of Christmas Day is often carried by the sound of excited children, choirs, and fuller than normal churches, Christmas Eve has more of the feel of wistfulness. We need to be sensitive to those who may have come to avoid the familiar faces of those who will gather in the morning. Perhaps they may be missing a part of their family. Perhaps one they loved has died and this is their first Christmas alone. Or perhaps every Christmas is a reminder that a special someone is not there, and there is no other time to be quiet, alone with deep thoughts.

For these, and a host of other reasons, the worship planners have to work hard to establish a worshipping community, one that will carry all the diverse emotions and expectations with which people will come.

In this particular service, an attempt is made to create contrasts between the joy of Christ's birth and the deeper feelings we have been identifying. The climax to the service is Holy Communion.
The service is carried by the carols. It is primarily a service of song. The prayers tend to carry the feeling of expectant joy. The others elements provide the contrast. In the Holy Communion, we are striving for a deeply spiritual moment. The sense, once again, is of the mystery of God, wondering at, as Charles Wesley put it, "our God contracted to a span, incomprehensibly made man."

Timing
Some congregations have a tradition of beginning their Christmas Eve late service at midnight. Others begin at 11:00 p.m., finishing at midnight with a Christmas greeting.
This service is designed to begin the Great Prayer of Thanksgiving at midnight, with a Christmas greeting. Some effort needs to be taken with timing to allow this to happen. The easiest variables to control will be the length of the address and the carols near to communion. The preacher may need a prompter if time is getting away from her or him. She or he may want to be in control of the carols to decide which will be added or deleted.

Sitting in silence for a minute or so as we wait for midnight can be helpful. It reminds us of the themes of Advent – a time of waiting – and gives us some space for personal preparation.

Decorations
If possible, the church will be candle-lit. Some kind of raised candelabras could be placed in the

aisles and in the sanctuary. All other lighting should be very soft, so that the candles provide some flickering effect. Seek to create an atmosphere of warmth and peace.

At the front of the worship space, an empty manger sits on the communion table. It can be slightly tilted toward the congregation so that the inside can be seen. If possible, softly spotlight it.

As people enter the church, each of them is given a small, 10 cm. (4 in.) long white candle, with a small square of cardboard surrounding it to protect fingers from hot wax.

For the communion, the glasses should be hidden from view until the table is set, or if a common cup is used, the wine/grape juice will be in a jug or decanter ready to pour at the same point.

The bread, chalice, and Christ candle are wrapped in a baby's shawl. The chalice and Christ candle form the baby's body; a round loaf of bread forms the head. The shawl is folded tightly around so that the elements are not visible. We want to create a surprise in the communion.

Below is a brief outline of comments and notes for the liturgy. It is then followed by the full liturgy.

Introduction
Quiet music is playing as people enter the church in candlelight. (Select some Christmas carols that are played quietly.) Announce at the beginning of the service that it will flow through without announcements.

You may want to explain the way in which communion will be received. (You may need to do this again at the point of the eucharistic liturgy.)

Processional
Three carols are sung at the beginning of the service. The third is the processional. The Bible is processed in followed by a woman carrying a baby wrapped in a shawl (the Christ candle, chalice and bread), then come the leader of worship, other participants (drama and soloists), and the preacher.

Choose people that represent the congregation: for example, a young person, an elderly person, a male, a female and others who represent the diversity of the congregation. The sense is one of awe, respect, and holiness.

Prayer of thanksgiving and invocation
An alternative to the responsive prayer provided might be to ask the worshippers what things they might want to give thanks for this year, and what hopes they have as they approach Christmas. These could be written up on an overhead projector transparency to form the basis of a prayer, or an extemporary prayer offered. The spirit is light and bright, led with good pace.

Scripture
The Dramatised Bible (1989, Marshall Pickering and Bible Society) provides a simple and more interesting way to present the readings. Otherwise, simply using a narrator and different voices for the characters will help with the presentation.

Contemporary reading/drama
There are a number of books that have excellent contemporary readings for Christmas (and other occasions). You will find a contemporary reading at the end of the section that may be useful, along with a brief drama.

Address
The theme will be the God who comes. Christmas Eve is a time of deep reflection, a time for remembering that God comes to us in gentle love. There is a sense of hope and openness, joy and expectation that real life and faith are possible.

The themes lend themselves to a reminder that the coming of Christ is the ultimate expression of God's covenant pledge to be with us forever. All of our longings are fulfilled in our relationship with God in Christ. Emphasize that God comes to us all, wherever we are at this point in time.

Carlo Carretto once wrote,
"To have found God, to have experienced [God] in the intimacy of our being, to have lived even for one hour in the fire of [God's] Trinity and the bliss of [God's] Unity clearly makes us say: "Now I understand. You alone are enough for me."[6]

The key to the theme will be the surprise of the elements for communion coming out of the manger on the communion table. It holds up the notion that the Christ who comes in the vulnerable babe is the one who continues to make himself vulnerable through his self-giving life of love, in his dying and rising, and by grace in the lives of the faithful.

Holy Communion
The communion will begin with a greeting at midnight. The lights are dimmed and the focus shifts to the manger.

Manipulate the timing by the selection of the carols. Two shorter carols that might be suitable after the address and prior to *Silent Night* (which sets the tone for the Eucharist) are *Infant Holy* and *Love Came Down at Christmas.* If it is near to midnight, sit for a short while in silence, to prepare for the sacrament.

You may want to explain the way in which the elements will be received prior to the singing of *Silent Night* and/or the time silence.

Different churches use varying liturgies. Insert your usual form, or adapt the one suggested.

As the solo *Cloth for the Cradle* is sung, the elements are slowly unwrapped from the shawl. The table is set, and finally the Christ candle is lit.

Receiving the elements
People are invited to come to the front of the worship area to receive the elements.

After being served, they are invited to light their candle from the Christ candle.

They may then return to their seat, or proceed to a prayer point where other candles may be lit and placed in a sand tray. There they may offer a personal prayer or simply place a lit candle in the tray as a sign of the hope that comes through Christ, the light of the world. (If there are particular prayer concerns in the congregation, or some focus of concern in the wider community, these could be highlighted at the beginning of the service.)

They then return to their seat with their candle lit from the Christ candle.

The lights remain dim to emphasize the spreading light of the candles.

Recessional
The last hymn, *Joy to the World,* is sung as the singing group leads the Christ light from the church, held high with a sense of reverence. The leaders of worship follow, then the whole congregation, symbolizing the taking of Christ's light out into the world.

For this service, you will need:
- worship leaders
- musicians
- singers
- two people for a drama
- preacher
- celebrant for Holy Communion
- Christ candle
- candles with drip protectors
- candle holders
- manger

CLOTH FOR THE CRADLE

Welcome and introduction

(The service will proceed without announcements of hymns, etc. Explain the way communion will be received and the lighting of the prayer candles. Invite participants to be thinking about prayers they may offer at that point.)

Carols   *O Little Town of Bethlehem*
Once in Royal David's City

Processional carol
The First Nowell

Call to worship

Come and immerse yourself in the mystery of Christmas;
Stop, pause, approach in silence,
For the long awaited has almost arrived.

Reflect on the wonder, on the miracle of birth;
Allow yourself to observe the scene,
The awe of those around.

See the star that heralds the holiest of events;
Listen to the angels proclaiming their song,
The joy of the birth of Christ.

Come and experience the eve that changed history;
Stop, pause, approach with reverence,
Our Saviour is here![7]

Prayer of thanksgiving & invocation

Leader: Loving God, who brought this world and all that is into being,
All: We gather to worship you in joyful celebration.

Leader: You have come among us with hope and love and mercy.
All: We praise you, loving Savior.

Leader: You have shown us that nothing will ever separate us from your love.
All: We worship you forever.

Leader:	You reach out to us, declaring that we are your own dear children.
All:	We bless your holy name.
Leader:	Come among us here tonight
All:	that we might know again the wonder of Christmas.
Leader:	Touch us.
All:	Renew us.
Leader:	Bless us.
All:	Make us yours and yours alone.
Leader:	In the name of Christ,
All:	For the sake of Christ,
Leader:	Amen.
All:	Yes – Amen.

Scripture   Isaiah 42:1–7
          Luke 2:1–20

Carols   *While Shepherds Watched*
          Angels from the Realms of Glory

Contemporary reading
          The best ever Christmas

Offering for the Christmas charity, offertory prayer, and prayer of intercession

(If your congregation has a special appeal for Christmas, then the offering might be directed there.)

The dedication of the offering will take the form of a prayer of intercession.

All giving and gracious God, you have provided your creation with all manner of good things.

We have all we need to care for this world and all its creatures, and you have provided us with food, shelter, and all we need to care for every person.

As we make this offering tonight, we are aware of the selfishness that denies the rights of the poor. We pray for those who will go hungry this Christmas.

We lift up those who will be alone, far from friends and family. We remember before you all who are suffering from disease, war, famine, or disaster. Dear God, let our offering be an expression of our desire that peace might reign in every land, and may the generosity of your people bring healing, comfort, and hope.

Merciful God, all about us there is so much hurt. Hear our silent prayers for those known personally to us – those you have placed upon our hearts at this time. (Silent prayer)

You alone can satisfy all human need, O God. Show us now where we can share in your Spirit's work, that all the world might know your blessing.
In the name of Christ, we pray. Amen.

Address

Solo & singing group

Silent Night

(Flute solo for one verse.
Singing group joins in to repeat verse one.)

Silent night! Holy night! All is calm, all is bright
round yon virgin mother and child.
Holy infant so tender and mild,
Sleep in heavenly peace, sleep in heavenly peace.

Flute, singing group and **congregation**

Silent night! Holy night! Shepherds quake at the sight:
glories stream from heaven afar,
Heavenly hosts sing Hallelujah
Christ the Savior is born, Christ the Savior is born.

Silent night! holy night! Son of God, love's pure light
radiant beams from thy holy face,
with the dawn of redeeming grace,
Jesus, Lord, at thy birth, Jesus, Lord, at thy birth.

Joseph Mohr
tr. John F. Young

Holy Communion

Leader:	It is Christmas day.
	The peace of God be with you.
All:	And also with you.

The congregation is invited to exchange the sign of peace using the same words.

The setting of the table

      (The elements are brought out as the solo is sung.)

Solo	Cloth for the Cradle, Cradle for the Child
	John L Bell and Graham Maule (From *Heaven Shall Not Wait*, W. G. R. G. Pearce Institute, Glasgow)

The Christ candle is lit

Leader:	The Lord be with you.
All:	And also with you.

Leader:	Lift up your hearts.
All:	We lift them to the Lord.

Leader:	Let us give thanks to the Lord our God.
All:	It is right to give our thanks and praise.

Leader:	We thank you, loving God, for in Christ you have come to dwell among us.
All:	You have made your home in our hearts; you have shared our life and entered our domain.

Leader:	We praise you for your affirming love.
All:	We thank you that you make us whole.

Leader:	When we deserved punishment,
All:	You offered freedom.

Leader:	When we were lost,
All:	You brought us home.

Leader:	Now we know that we belong to you forever.
All:	And so we praise you with all the company of heaven, rejoicing in one voice:
	Holy, holy, holy Lord, God of power and might,

Heaven and earth are full of your glory,
Hosannah in the highest.
Blessed be the one who comes in the name of the Lord.
Hosannah in the highest.

Leader: You call us to this feast this night, O Lord. You are the host, and we are privileged to be here. By your word and through your grace, we are fed and nurtured. Let your Spirit come upon us, and may this bread and wine be transformed into the food of eternal life.

Remember that on the night of his betrayal, Jesus took bread, and when he had given thanks, he broke it and gave it to the disciples saying: "Take, eat, this is my body which is broken for you. Do this in remembrance of me."

Then again, after supper, he took the cup and said: "This is my blood of the new covenant. It is shed for you and for many for the forgiveness of sins. Drink from this, all of you."

Gracious Savior, in this meal we would know perfect communion with you. In the eating of this bread and the drinking of this wine, may we be one forever.

All: May we be one, lost in love forever, until the end of the age.

Leader: In faith and hope, we pray the prayer our Savior has taught us:
All: Our father in heaven,
hallowed be your name,
your kingdom come,
your will be done,
on earth as in heaven.
Give us today our daily bread.
Forgive us our sins
as we forgive those who sin against us.
Save us from the time of trial
and deliver us from evil.
For the kingdom, the power, and the glory are yours
now and forever. Amen.

(The congregation is invited to come to the front to receive the elements. They may then proceed to light a candle from the Christ candle, and if they wish, to move to the prayer point to light a second candle as a sign of hope and peace. Feel free to spend awhile there in prayer.)

Prayer after Communion

Leader: You have fed and nurtured us by word and sacrament, O God. Now, empower us by your Spirit to live to your glory, to serve in your name, to bring justice and freedom for all.

All: In the name of Jesus, our savior and Lord. Amen

Carol   *Joy to the World*

(The leaders of worship will lead the congregation out as a sign that Christ is truly the light of the world).

The best ever Christmas

Times were hard. Ed and Eve had moved to a "one-horse town" in the middle of nowhere with their kids, Ed Jr. and Marg. It was a totally isolated place, mostly red dust, a train line, and a few buildings. Ed was away most of the time, working on the trains. In fact, the only way he'd get home was when one train dropped him off before another picked him up.

The high-pitched shrill of a train whistle in the distance always stirred the family one way or another – excitement or dread, it was a familiar cycle. Perhaps the worst time came just two days before Christmas. They had been promised a week's holiday together, but old Jack had gone on a bender, and no one knew exactly where he'd gone to – hitched a ride on the petrol tankers bound for Broken Hill perhaps?

The phone had rung, and the demand laid down, and Ed was gone. When would he be back? A few days, maybe a week!

Christmas without Dad – the tears flowed like a torrent. Marg was inconsolable. Little Ed bit his lip and tried to be strong, but everything seemed so black.

Eve did her best. The decorations tried in vain to brighten the house. An extra place was set for lunch as though they could conjure Dad up in their imaginations, and all Christmas morning she sang carols at the top of her voice. Marg busied herself, helping with the vegies, but Ed just sat on the verandah looking up the line that had taken his father away.

Noon came, and Eve called him in to wash for lunch. He stood to enter the tiny kitchen that had the only running water in the house. Just then, a small black dot on the line caught his eye. A crow, perhaps, pecking at some kill on the track? No, too big for a bird – maybe a kangaroo.

He sat down again and watched it come, growing bigger with the moments. Then he saw it. That familiar gate and roll of the shoulders.

"Mum! Mum! Come and look! It's Dad. Dad's come home for Christmas!"

Sure enough, there he was, wet through from the walk, all large as life and whistling *While Shepherds Watched*.

All three ran down the line and Ed quickened his step a bit, too tired even to jog. There in the middle of nowhere, they formed a tangle of arms and legs, tears, hugs, and kisses.

It was the best Christmas ever. Three hours there, three hours back, in the stinking heat of an Aussie summer – for just one hour's lunch. Crazy maybe – but love will do that to you every time.

BORN IN US
A Christmas Day service

This service centers on the idea that the incarnation recurs in each of us as we allow Christ to be born again in our lives. It features a number of characters from history. You may choose to have them dress in period costume or depict them as people just like us.

As Christmas Day is a day of high emotion, the style of the service is deliberately simple, featuring choirs and soloists. Some music has been suggested, but many congregations will choose their own familiar pieces.

For this service, you will need:
- worship leaders
- musicians
- choir and soloists
- preacher
- people for the dramas

BORN IN US

Prelude

Greeting

Leader:	May the peace, joy, and blessing of Christ's coming be with you.
People:	And also with you.

Leader:	Let us worship the Christ, the incarnate Word of God.
People:	Let us celebrate his birth – God, come amongst us.

Leader:	Let us sing songs of praise
People:	And shout with joy unto the Lord.

Leader:	Let the name of Jesus be praised.
People:	Let him be adored forever.

Processional:

O Come Adore Him, by Franz Schubert

Prayer of praise and adoration

Glorious God, who is born among us, we praise and worship you this day. You share our humanity; you enter into the struggle of our lives, bringing us life and love. We thank you for your presence, here with us now. We praise you for the gift of your Spirit, the Spirit of Christ born among us.

You make yourself vulnerable for the sake of our salvation. You put yourself into the hands of frail humans, and trust us to care. You show us all what we can be, inviting humankind to be loving, faithful, and just.

Receive our adoration, for you overwhelm us with love and grace. May our worship honor you. May we delight you with our praise. May our words, thoughts, and songs bring you pleasure. In the name of Christ we pray. Amen.

Carol   *The First Nowell*

Reading   Luke 2:1–7

Mary & Joseph

Carol   *Love came down at Christmas*

Reading   Luke 2:8–14

Choir   *Angels We Have Heard on High*, by John Ness Beck

Julian of Norwich

Reading   Luke 2:15–20

Choir   *Benedictus*, by Darros

John Wesley

Christmas charity offering & Intercessory prayer

Offertory   *African Noel*, by Victor Johnson *(Sung by the men of the choir.)*

Dedication of offering

Leader: To the glory of God, for the sake of the world,
People: We dedicate this offering Lord.

Leader: To the glory of God, for the sake of the world,
People: We dedicate our lives to your service.

Prayers for the World
Let us pray for our world.

Come, O come Emmanuel, God with us. Come into our world with peace and hope, joy and salvation. Come, O Light Eternal, shine in the dark and fearsome places where hearts are hard and life is cheap, and too many are made to count the cost.
Come, Spirit of Life, pour out your healing power upon all who will, this day, cry out in anguish at the injustice heaped upon them. Come, Savior of the world, and set us free.

Prayers for the church
Let us pray for the church.

We are your people, called by your name, to be a servant people for the sake of the world. We come before you, seeking the gifts of your Spirit, that we may reflect your loving kindness in the ministries we offer. Grant us your compassion, Lord, that we might never turn our back on another. Grant us tolerance, Lord, that we might see the best in another. Grant us your love, Lord, that our hearts may embrace others in your name. Grant us your strength, Lord, that we may be filled with passion for the gospel.

We are your people, called by your name; make us like you, we pray.

Duet   *And He Shall Feed His Flock*, by Handel

Prayers for those in neen

Let us pray for those in need.

Merciful God, whose will is to save and heal, hear us as we pray for those known to us who are in need of your healing touch this day. As we name them in the silence, may your Spirit bring mercy and grace to meet their needs.
(Silent prayer)
Your grace is sufficient for every situation. Leave us now confident of your power to save, and show us where we can be used in these lives. In the name of Christ we pray. Amen.

The Lord's Prayer

All: Our Father in heaven,
hallowed be your name,
your kingdom come,
your will be done,
on earth as in heaven.
Give us today our daily bread.
Forgive us our sins
as we forgive those who sin against us.
Save us from the time of trial
and deliver us from evil.
For the kingdom, the power, and the glory are yours
now and forever. Amen.

Carol   *Hark! The Herald Angels Sing*

Dietrich Bonhoeffer

Address

Carol   *Joy to the World*

Blessing

May the love of God fill our hearts.
May the grace of Christ keep us true.
May the peace of the Spirit make us strong
And may the Spirit of the Christ-child fill us with joy.
Now and forever. Amen.

Postlude

Monologues for Christmas Day

Mary and Joseph

Joseph: My name is Joseph and this is my wife, Mary.

Mary: *We are humble folks.*

Joseph: I am a carpenter from Nazareth... nothing special... We are just an ordinary couple.

Mary: *But God does not seem to mind mixing with folk like us... but then you know the story well by now!*

Joseph: What is not written, though, is how scared we were...

Mary: *and confused...*

Joseph: and if I was honest, full of doubt.
Well, wouldn't you be? Angelic visitations, my wife pregnant before we... well... you know!
And told that he was to be the one promised long ago... the Messiah... the Son of God!

Mary: *It is a strange thing... even though it still frightens me to think about it... I always knew it would be all right... in here, you know, I always was sure in here!*

Joseph: Through all those years, as he grew and learned, full of questions, full of passion... what a responsibility. But this I always knew; if God had chosen us, then we must be worthy, and therefore able.

Mary: *That's right, no matter what, we always knew God was with us. What love! What goodness! What hope he gave.*

Joseph: You could not be near him without sensing it. You could not hear him speak without knowing... he was the truth.

Mary: *And God chose us...*

Joseph: What a privilege!

Julian of Norwich

My name is Julian. I lived in the 14th century in Norwich. Like many women of my day, I was an Anchoress, seeking solace in the order of prayer and meditation. I loved the daily cycle of prayer. I loved the quiet moments of reflection and the beauty of worship.

My life was simple... unremarkable...

Then one day in May, 1373, all that changed. God chose me... me... to bring a message of hope to our dark and frightening world.

There, where friend and foe alike were being cut down by the scourge we called Black Death, where young and old waited grimly for the bearer's wagon to take them to their grave, there God spoke to me in a series of revelations... clear as day... loud as the Crier's call they came...overwhelming... compulsive... decisive.

He showed me a little thing, the size of a hazelnut, on the palm of my hand, round like a ball. I looked at it thoughtfully and wondered, "What is it?" And the answer came, "It is all that is made." I marveled that it continued to exist and did not suddenly disintegrate; it was so small. And again my mind supplied the answer, "It exists both now and forever, because God loves it."

And therein I saw three truths: the first is that God made it; the second is that God loves it; and the third is that God sustains it.

And so it is with us, our body, mind, and soul. God will not let us go. We shall not perish. In Christ is salvation. In him we have our life... our being ... our all.

John Wesley

My name is John Wesley.

I was an Anglican priest who lived in the 18th century.

Until I was 35 years of age, I knew there was something lacking in my life. I had been part of many groups; the best known of them was the Holy Club at Oxford. Always, always, always, I was looking for one thing – to know God – personally, intimately and to know Jesus Christ as my Savior and Lord.

No amount of rigor, method, prayer, or study sufficed. I could not find that faith for which I longed so much.

Then, on May 24th, 1738, in Aldersgate Street, it happened. I felt my heart warmed with the inner glow of the Spirit, and I knew I *did* trust in Christ, and Christ alone for my salvation; an assurance was given me that he had taken away my sins, even mine, and saved me from the law of sin and death.

For the next 50 years I purposed to tell the world of this wonderful Savior. From England to the Americas I sang, preached, and argued for the souls of others. The movement I began has now spread to the four corners of the earth. I could never have imagined it would be so... but let this be known... it is not the Methodist Church or our hymns for which I would be remembered... No!... Only this Christ is God's means of salvation... and in him alone can we trust.
God is love, and in Christ we have seen salvation. May he be glorified forever!

Dietrich Bonhoeffer

My name is Dietrich – Dietrich Bonhoeffer.

Many of you will know of me. Some may even remember me.

What a life I have lived.

Ahhh, those early years, growing up in the midst of things, in the center of culture, at the heart of learning, mixing with the greatest Christian minds. It was wonderful, breathtaking, and delightful. My career seemed assured – lecturer, pastor, teacher – in the old language, a prince of the confessing church!
How could I have ever known?
He was literally like a thief in the night, creeping up upon me, overtaking me, demanding of *me* the faith I had proclaimed in him. He changed everything. No longer an academic pursuit, this Jesus demanded of me a righteousness, a life lived out in faith and courage.

In the face of that worm Hitler and his henchmen, how could I be silent?
And in the face of my church's quietude, how could I turn my back?
Whether the plot to kill Hitler was right or wrong, you be the judge.
This is all I know... in Christ I found my life, and in that life I found the cause of justice, and in that cause I found true faith! Though it did cost me my life upon that scaffold, I would not change a thing.

Each of us must face the decisive moment – that moment when you know it is all or nothing. What does life amount to if it is but days lived out without a cause, without a meaning? Do I regret it all? Not a moment! To live is Christ, to die is gain!

Chapter four

Party Time

New Year's Eve

Landmarks in life and history encourage us to leave the past behind and beckon us forward to a new beginning. A new millennium, a new century, and a new decade, is a new beginning. The dawn of the New Year has always had something of a sense of an opportunity to turn over a new leaf, and to shape the future. Amongst the anxiety associated with the unknown, there is always a sense of humanity having an opportunity to turn over a new leaf, corporately and individually. Movements such as Jubilee 2000 call us forward to a different kind of world in which Third World debt is forgiven. As well as being reminded of some of the great atrocities, failings, and devastation of the past years, we are also reminded of some of the great advances we have made and the great humanitarian acts performed.

For many people, New Year's Eve is a time of great loneliness where they are not comfortable in being in some of the places where the community gathers. While "everyone" is out partying, they feel alone with nowhere to go and no one to connect with. New Year's Eve worship services are a strong tradition in some congregations. They offer an opportunity to confirm the route which life is following as well as making some important, direction-shaping decisions in the context of worship. People can be invited to bring friends and relatives, and even the local neighborhood can be invited. The services can be early in the evening, followed by a party, perhaps at the church. Alternatively there can be a party, meal, or dance first, and then people can move into the church to hold a Covenant Service at midnight.

From the old to the new – an informal gathering

If your congregation is planning a party, watchnight service, or retreat, it might be helpful to symbolize the transition from the old to the new year.

Some groups may like to gather at dusk. A brazier containing live coals might be already alight as they gather. (Ensure there are many more coals than participants.)

The group is invited to recall some of the inventions and new technologies that have been developed in the 20th century and early 21st century.

Spontaneous prayers, one from the orders of service or a prayer such as the following could be offered:

> *Loving God, so much has been developed in our lifetime that we marvel at the creative genius you have instilled in your children. We offer praise and thanks for all that makes our life comfortable, rich, and full, and we pray that we might never take your blessings for granted.*

Again, the group might be invited to share things that have happened in the 20th century and early 21st century that have brought shame, pain, and terror.

Again, spontaneous prayers, one from the orders of service or a prayer such as the following, could be offered:

> *We recall, with shame, all that humanity has committed that has brought death and destruction to your creation. We are sorry for our foolish pride and wilful arrogance that has turned us from your will and care. Have mercy on us, O God.*

Let us name the things we have identified… (People call out their concerns.)

> After each one, the response
>
> *Lord, have mercy.*
> **Lord, have mercy.**

may be offered, or at the end, the traditional three-part response may be offered:

> *Lord, have mercy.*
> **Lord, have mercy.**
>
> *Christ, have mercy.*
> **Christ, have mercy.**
>
> *Lord, have mercy.*
> **Lord, have mercy.**

When the prayers are concluded, a few of the coals are taken from the brazier, removed, and put in a smaller urn or dish. Participants are then invited to reflect on those things that they might like to deal with from the past as quiet music is played. (These could be relationship problems, actions, concerns or fears, unsatisfactory traits, or unresolvable problems.) When they are ready, invite the group to come forward, and using metal tongs, place one of the coals from the original brazier in a receptacle, offering the words:

> *I turn from the past to embrace the future God is giving me.*

During the night, the remaining coals/embers are kept alight by the group, using one or two additional pieces of coal as necessary. These symbolize that the past is always with us, shaping us and creating the future.

At dawn (or at midnight if that is to be the end of the evening), the embers are fanned into flame, more coals are added to create a blazing fire.

Prayers for the future are then offered by the group.

The Covenant Prayer found below could be said, or spontaneous prayers offered, or one person could lead the group using the following:

> *God of the ages, who gives each day its light, and fills it with life and love, open to us the future you desire for your children. As we turn toward the new dawn's horizon, fill us with your gifts of faith, hope, and love. Enable us to embrace all that is before us with the certain knowledge that you are there with us. May the future bring justice, mercy, community, and goodness. May we live to your glory, for the sake of Christ. Amen.*

> *"What does the Lord require of you but to do justice, and to love kindness, and to walk humbly with your God?"* (Micah 6:8)

(If you live in a place where fires are dangerous, the same effects can be achieved with candles. If it is possible to use fire, it lends itself to a barbecued breakfast. Recounting stories of the resurrected Jesus gathering on the shore to eat fish might serve as a reminder that Christ is with us, in which case the breakfast could be fish and bread.)

IT'S PARTY TIME

Below, you will find two quite different worship services. The first creates more of a party atmosphere. The second is a more reflective service in the tradition of John Wesley's Covenant Service. Holy Communion may be included as a part of the second service in whatever form you use in your tradition. These services may be used on New Year's Eve, the first Sunday of the new year or at a time in January when things are getting underway again following holidays. They may also be adapted slightly and used as services where leaders are dedicated or new steps in faith are celebrated.

For this service, you will need:
- a worship leader
- two readers for *The Paradox of Our Time*
- a supply of party poppers and streamers distributed throughout the church underneath chairs or pews
- visual images of the third millennium and the 20th century

Present visual images of the past year and the year ahead while Psalm 8 is being read. You will find resources for the images on various clip art services, some of which can be found on the Internet. Ensure that no copyright is breached by taking images from magazines, books, or other sources without permission.

IT'S PARTY TIME

Call to worship

> Here and now, God invites us to a new day.
> Through Christ we are invited to a new beginning.
> The Holy Spirit breaks into our lives to inspire us and beckon us forward.

Song　　*Father Welcomes All His Children*
　　　　　　In the House of God

The Paradox of Our Time – a message from the Internet
(To be read by two voices from different parts of the church, or by the congregation divided into left- and right-hand sides.)

> The paradox of our time in history is that we have taller buildings, but shorter tempers;
> *wider freeways, but narrower viewpoints.*
> We spend more, but have less;
> *we buy more, but enjoy it less.*
> We have bigger houses and smaller families;
> *more conveniences, but less time.*
> We have more degrees, but less sense;
> *more knowledge, but less judgment;*
> more experts, but more problems;
> *more medicine, but less wellness.*
>
> We have multiplied our possessions, but reduced our values.
> *We talk too much, love too seldom, and hate too often.*
> We've learned how to make a living, but not a life;
> *we've added years to life, not life to years.*
>
> We've been all the way to the moon and back, but have trouble crossing the street to meet the new neighbor.
> *We've conquered outer space, but inner space remains a mystery.*
> We've cleaned up the air, but polluted the soul;
> *we've split the atom, but not our prejudice.*
> We have higher incomes, but lower morals;
> *we've grown long on quantity, but short on quality.*

These are the times of tall people, with short character;
  steep profits, and shallow relationships.
These are the times of striving for world peace, but domestic warfare;
  more leisure, but less fun; more kinds of food, but less nutrition.

These are days of two incomes, but more divorce;
  of fancier houses, but broken homes.

All: It is a time when technology can send this message around the world in an instant, and a time when you can choose either to make a difference, or to just hit delete...

Song   *Comfort, Comfort All My People*

Absolution

My little children, I am writing these things to you so that you may not sin. But if anyone does sin, we have an advocate with God, Jesus Christ the righteous; and he is the atoning sacrifice for our sins, and not for ours only but also for the sins of the whole world. (1 John 2:1, 2, *An Inclusive Language Lectionary*)

So I declare to you:
Our sins are forgiven.
Thanks be to God.

A Prayer of Thanksgiving
(Invite people to throw the streamers or pop the poppers they will find under their seats at the conclusion of a paragraph of the prayer when they choose.)

Loving God of this and every new beginning,
we give you thanks for your faithfulness and protection throughout
  all generations.
Even when our technological advances have been used to
  destructive ends,
you have saved us from destroying your world and ourselves.

We give you thanks for the advances in human achievement;
for the way medical technology has brought healing and eased
  pain;
for the advances in agriculture, food production, and water supply;
for the removal of slavery and the increases in communication;
for the beauty of music and art, of dance and of drama.

We give you thanks for the times ignorance has been overcome;
for education and great minds that have liberated and enlight-
    ened us;
for the increased inclusion of young people, women, and differ-
    ently abled people;
for the invention of printing presses, telephones, and computers;
for photography, video, and increased news services.

We thank you for your gift of faith and hope.
Even in times of disillusionment, people have kept striving for
    peace, justice, and civil rights.
Oppression and lawlessness have continued to be overcome, com-
    munity and unity have been developed and grown, and your
    good news has spread throughout the earth.

(Here you might like to invite people to call out in single words or phrases
    the things that they are thankful for, as follows.)

And now, God, we would offer these words and phrases that
    represent the thanks of our hearts and minds. Please feel free
    to call them out in a loud voice.

So, God, if we were to thank you for all the things that you have
    done, we would be here recounting your blessings to us for
    ages to come.
Now as we come to a new year, in anticipation and hope we give
    you thanks for the good times yet to come.
May our lives live the thanks and give you the praise.
Amen.

Images of the year past

Prayers for others and prayers for our world

Invite people to share for two or three minutes with one or two other people their hopes
for other people and for the world in the year ahead. Invite people to share these hopes
as one-sentence prayers prayed aloud in the congregation. Introduce and conclude the
prayer as follows:

Sovereign God, we bring you our prayers for the world and for
    other people, hear now our prayers.

Receive the prayers and the longings of our hearts. Amen.

Song   *Spirit of Peace*
            Prayer of St. Francis

Reflection *Share a brief reflection that invites people to a new beginning. One possibility is included at the end of the services – the story* The Little Boy and the Circus.

Song   *Power of Your Love*
            Here I Am, Lord

Benediction

A new day dawns and God the Creator invites us forward into the future. Go, being assured of the companionship of Christ and the sustaining power of the Holy Spirit.

SERVICE FOR COVENANT AND RENEWAL

For this service, you will need:

- small candles or tapers to give to people as they enter the church
- a Christ candle lit at the front of the church
- worship leader
- preparation for Holy Communion if you are planning to include this in the service.

Provide an atmosphere of quiet and reverence, perhaps with dimmed lighting or light from candles filling the church. Ensure there is enough light for people to be able to read the prayers.

SERVICE FOR COVENANT AND RENEWAL

Call to worship: *(read responsively)*

O, Lord, you have searched me and known me.
You know when I sit down and when I rise up.
You discern my thoughts from far away.
You search out my path and my lying down,
and are acquainted with all my ways.
Even before a word is on my tongue,
Oh Lord you know it completely.
You hem me in, behind and before,
and lay your hand on me.

All: In awe, wonder, and praise, we worship you and come to offer our lives anew.

Song   *The Great Love of God*

Prayer of confession

A thousand pardons, Lord!

(This prayer might be divided amongst the congregation for reading.)

Come, let us unburden ourselves.

Let us pray.

Gracious and loving God,
we would bring our prayers of confession.
We bring all that needs confessing from our history, O God –
a history of wars, of greed, of lust for power and of domination.
We bring a history of abuse, of racism, of injustice,
of colonization, and of destruction and oppression of indigenous peoples
and their lands.
We bring a history of inequality, of sustained poverty and deficiency.
At the end of a year, Lord, we beg a thousand pardons.

Gracious and loving God,
in confession we bring to you our lack of love for others.
We bring the hardening of hearts.
With our increased development of worldwide media coverage
has come increased awareness of those in need,
but we have used the remote control to change the channel,
escaping from channels of reality to channels of pleasure and fantasy.
At the end of a year, Lord, we beg a thousand pardons.

Gracious and loving God,
we have taken the gift of creativity,
and with it we have increased our productivity but not our character,
our Gross National Product but not our generosity,
our technological possibilities,
but not our compassionate opportunities,
our receptivity to respectability, but not to our responsibility.
At the end of a year, Lord, we beg a thousand pardons.

Gracious and loving God,
at the end of this past year,
we confess that our busyness has overtaken us,
and we have crowded you out, as we have crowded out the time to
reflect and evaluate.
Our lifestyles have focussed on our wants and ourselves.
So often we have forgotten you, the giver of life and peace,
of joy and patience, of kindness, faithfulness and loyalty.
At the end of a year, Lord, we beg a thousand pardons.

Gracious and loving God,
even as we come to beg your pardon,
we hear and experience the refreshment of good news.
When we have forgotten you, you have not forgotten us.
You have remained faithful and just,
and have brought us to a new year,
to a new beginning,
with forgiveness and renewed hope.

At the end of a year, God,
you bring us more than a thousand, thousand pardons
and our hearts and spirits cry out with all of your people:
Thanks be to God unto all eternity.

Hymn   *O God, Our Help in Ages Past*

Prayer for our mission
> *Invite people to stand and name aspects of mission in which they are in-volved, for example, hospital visitation, ministry with children, Meals on Wheels. As each mission is described the leader says:*
> God of all ages and times,
>
> *and the congregation responds:*
> grow our service and mission for the sake of your gospel.

Scripture sentences
> John 10:10
> Romans 12:1–3
> 2 Corinthians 5:17

Reflection *Share a brief reflection that shares what Christ has done for us and the invitation we have to new life. One possible story –* The Little Boy and the Circus *– is included at the end of the services.*

Hymn　　　*Jesus, You Have Come to the Lakeshore*

Covenant prayer

Introduction

Lord Jesus Christ, you have made us your own, and once more we
　　offer ourselves in your witness and service.
I am no longer my own, but yours.

I am no longer my own, but yours.
Put me to what you will,
Rank me with who you will;
Put me to doing, put me to suffering;
Let me be employed for you or laid aside for you;
Exalted for you or brought low for you;
Let me be full, let me be empty;
Let me have all things, let me have nothing;
I freely and wholeheartedly yield all things to your pleasure and
　　disposal.

And now, glorious and blessed God,
Father, Son and Holy Spirit,
You are mine, and I am yours
Amen.

From *Uniting in Worship*, Uniting Church Press, Melbourne, 1988.
Used by permission.

*Following the covenant prayer, invite people to come forward with their
candle to the front of the church for prayer. People may wish to stand or to
kneel. Elders or leaders of the congregation may stand on one side and be
available to pray with people should they desire this. Following their time
of prayer, people light their candle from a Christ candle and return to
their seats.*

*If you plan to include communion as a part of this service, include what-
ever prayers and words of preparation are your usual tradition and invite
people to share in communion when they come forward to pray and light
their candle.*

Hymn:　　　*Have Faith in God, My Heart*

The Little Boy and the Circus

A little boy who lived in an isolated country in the late 1800s had reached the age of 12 and had never in all his life seen a circus. He loved all the things he heard about the circus. He would get books out of the school library and beg his parents to read it to him. You can imagine his excitement when, one day, posters went up around the town announcing that on the next Saturday a traveling circus was coming to the nearby town. He ran home as fast as his little legs would carry him. He asked his mum if he could go, but she said, "Ask your father when he comes home!"

As soon as he heard his father coming, he raced out with the glad news and the question, "Daddy, can I go?" Although the family was poor, the father sensed how important this was to the lad.

"If you do your Saturday chores ahead of time," he said, "I'll see to it that you have the money to go."

Come Saturday morning, the chores were done and the little boy stood by the breakfast table, dressed in his Sunday best. His father reached down into the pocket of his overalls and pulled out a dollar bill, the most money the little boy had possessed at one time in all his life. The father cautioned him to be careful and then sent him on his way to town. The boy was so excited, his feet hardly seemed to touch the ground all the way. As he neared the outskirts of the village, he noticed people lining the streets. He worked his way through the crowd until he could see what was happening. Lo and behold, it was the approaching spectacle of a circus parade!

The parade was the grandest thing the boy had ever seen. Caged animals snarled as they passed, bands beat their rhythms and sounded shining horns. Midgets performed acrobatics while flags and ribbons swirled overhead. He saw the clowns which he thought were funnier than he could ever have imagined. Finally, after everything had passed where he was standing, the traditional ringmaster with black boots, white pants and a red coat brought up the rear. As the ringmaster passed by, the little boy reached into his pocket and took out that precious dollar bill. Handing the money to the ringmaster, the boy turned around and went home.

What had happened? The boy thought he had seen the circus but had only seen the parade! He missed the real thing!

Chapter five

The Passion of Love

Holy Week to Easter

For Christians, the most sacred of all the seasons is Easter. Like Christmas, it is permeated with many secular values and customs. It is also so well known by the secular culture in which we live that there is a real challenge for worship leaders to create something new and interesting that will break through the complacency of many.

The services in this section invite participants to journey with Jesus through the events of Easter. Beginning with a service of Tenebrae, there are opportunities to reflect on the Last Supper through a Passover re-enactment; experience something of the depths of Christ's pain and the pain of the world on Good Friday; and have our spirits raised in the joy of the resurrection.

Be patient

One sometimes has the impression that preachers, aware that there are many worshippers who come only at Easter and Christmas, strive too hard to "get the message across." One of the most obvious outcomes is the tendency to get to Easter Sunday on Friday or in Holy Week. There are many ways to invite worshippers into the story. For centuries, Christians have used drama, cantatas, and other creative arts to convey the message.

These services seek to tell the story, little by little. The object is to leave the participant where the story is, rather than offer the complete gospel at each service. We seek to help worshippers experience each component at depth as we enter into the mystery of those saving acts.

Visuals

Years of worshipping in one environment can deaden the senses to the symbols always present. Beautiful stained glass and banners lose some of their impact, simply because we take them for granted. During the high festivals of faith, particular attention should be given to visual symbols. These are ideal times to highlight a symbol, or develop new ways of focusing our faith.

In the Tenebrae service, which highlights the betrayal of Christ, a large candelabra with seven candles sits on the communion table. The table may be dressed in black cloth. If possible, the lights are dimmed progressively so that, as each of the candles is extinguished, one has the sense of the encircling gloom of Christ's circumstance.

The Passover re-enactment can be held at the church or in the home. If it is at home, the participants could share the meal reclining on cushions on the floor in the fashion of the Middle Eastern customs of Jesus' day. Or one might want to have a more contemporary feel, and set up the room as a dinner party. If the re-enactment is held at the church, a hall could be decorated to have the feel of a restaurant. Use your imagination to make it live.

Many churches have the custom of decorating the church with black cloth on Good Friday. Sometimes it is done prior to worship so that people come to worship and the impact is immediate. On other occasions, the church is "dressed" during the worship as the full horror of the crucifixion unfolds. Some churches have no instrumental music apart from the hymns. Others may want to leave the lights turned off to create an atmosphere of gloom. The worship leaders may dress fully in black, to reinforce the effect.

On Easter Sunday, it is a different story. In the liturgy provided here, it is suggested that we pick up the theme as we left it Friday. Not until the trumpet fanfare and the call to worship, "Christ is risen!" does the transformation occur. The goal is to convey the movement from death to life, from the tomb to the garden, from the crucifixion to the resurrected Christ.

The first time this happened at one particular church, the young minister was pulled aside by a very disgruntled elderly woman who said, "Young man, are you the only person in the entire country who does not know what day it is?" "Be patient, you'll see!" came the reply. Afterwards she simply said, "I got the point! Thank you."

So, to the particular services.

TENEBRAE
The service of shadows

Introduction
This service is one of the oldest traditions of the Christian church for the celebration of Holy Week. The word "tenebrae" comes from the Latin and means "shadows." Therefore the service has become known as the **service of shadows**.

During the course of the worship, as the successive chapters in the story of Christ's passion are read, the candles and lights of the church are extinguished one by one until, finally, only one candle is left burning. Thus, as the passion story unfolds, the darkness increases until we near the death of our Lord: only one candle is left burning – the light of God's love. This light is carried from the church symbolizing our Lord's three days in the tomb.

On Easter Sunday, the Christ light again becomes a focus of worship

Symbolism

A seven-stick candelabra (corresponding to a Jewish menorah) provides an excellent focus in the sanctuary of the church. An outer candle is successively extinguished after each of the first six readings, leaving only the central candle alight after the seventh reading. If practicable, the candelabra (with only one candle burning) can be processed out of the church at the end of the service.

Other symbols representative of the crucifixion are also very suitable. For instance, a large wooden cross, a purple cloak, a crown of thorns, and heavy nails.

Organization

For the dramatic impact of this service to be conveyed successfully to the congregation, much thought must be given to the overall "theme" (this will in turn influence the choice of music, and also the items presented between the seven readings).

Additionally, the service of Tenebrae is very visual. The flow of presentations must be carefully managed, as must the availability of dwindling light for readers, musicians, etc. Thought must also be given to the safety of older people leaving the church in darkness (perhaps a foyer light could be switched on after the service is concluded).

This service lends itself to a number of uses. Some churches may want to use it during Holy Week, to begin the season. Others might use it on Maundy Thursday, while others will use it on Good Friday. The choice of readings will differ, depending on the timing.

Alternative readings:

Early in the week	Thursday	Friday
1. John 11:4 –53	Matthew 26:1–16	Luke 23:32–38
2. John 12:27–37	Matthew 26:36–46	John 19:22–7
3. Matthew 26:1–16	Matthew 26:47–56	Luke 23:39–43
4. Matthew 26:36–46	Matthew 26:57–66	Matthew 27:45–49
5. Matthew 26:47–56	Matthew 26:69–75	John 19:28–29
6. Matthew 26:69–75	Matthew 27:11–23	John 19:30, Matthew 27:51
7. Matthew 27:20–26	Matthew 27:24–31	Luke 23:44–49

For this service, you will need:

- readers
- liturgists
- musicians
- recorded music
- audiovisual
- candelabra
- lighting control

TENEBRAE

Musical prelude

Approximately five minutes of wistful/contemplative music is played as the congregation arrives.

Introduction

A description of the service (as per the "overview" above, or similar).

Congregational hymn

O Sacred Head, Sore Wounded

FIRST LESSON

Leader: Hear the story of the passion of our Lord and of his rejection by the religious authorities as they plotted against Jesus.
(John 11:45–53 is read.)

The first candle is extinguished.

Prayer Most merciful God, who comes to us no matter what our circumstance, we come to you – a people who dwell in an era of cruelty and injustice.

We would look for the light, but it is overshadowed by the hostility and hatred of selfish ambition.

We long for peace, but there are those whose lust for power oppresses humankind.

We desire justice, but find instead intolerance, racism, and violence.

Where can we turn, O God? Who will plead the cause of the powerless?

Our hope is solely in you. You are the only one we can trust. You alone are faithful and true.

Heal our world. Heal our broken hearts. Heal our wounded spirits, we pray. In the name of the one who takes on all our pain, Jesus the Christ. Amen.

Choir/solo *O Lord, Hear My Prayer* by Jaques Berthier

SECOND LESSON

Leader: Hear the story of the passion of our Lord and of his betrayal by Judas.
(Matthew 26 :1–16 is read.)

The second candle is extinguished.

Poem   *The night he was betrayed* by Margaret Knauerhase.

"The night he was betrayed he broke the bread."
Tonight? Last night? Two thousand years ago?
"Do this in memory of me," he said.
Can we forget a thing we do not know?

We do not know, though saints have bravely spoken,
We do not wish to know, for that implies
Response to blood spilled and to body broken,
Unwearying love, service and sacrifice.

This is the age of comfort, and the day
Of "our own thing," the all-important "I,"
The self-assuring, self-expressing way.
What can it mean to us, who still pass by?

And yet, and yet a wistful voice within us
Whispers unwillingly and half-afraid,
"He loves us, suffers, gives himself to win us."
O God, which was the night he was betrayed?

Congregational hymn
When My Love to Christ Grows Weak

THIRD LESSON
Leader: Hear the story of the passion of our Lord and of his agony and
arrest in the garden.
(Matthew 26:36–56 is read.)

The third candle is extinguished.

Sacred dance
A short dance (two to three minutes) perhaps incorporating symbols
associated with the crucifixion (for example, crown of thorns, nails,
and chalice).
and/or
Choir/solo *Bitter Was the Night* by Sydney Carter

FOURTH LESSON
Leader: Hear the story of the passion of our Lord and of his trial before
Caiaphas the High Priest.
(Matthew 26:57–75 is read.)

The fourth candle is extinguished.

Poem   *I plucked a bramble* by Margaret Knauerhase.

> I plucked a bramble by the temple wall.
> The moon shone white upon the ancient town.
> It scratched my hand – I watched the dark drops fall,
> But still I plaited it into a crown,
> And men were harsh and crueller than now –
> They jammed it fiercely on his patient brow.
>
> He spoke no word of anger or of blame.
> Beneath the blood his steady eyes looked down.
> I am quite sure he never heard my name,
> And yet he knew that I had made the crown.
> His long look I shall see to my life's end –
> He looked at me as if I were his friend.
>
> The scratches on my hands have never healed,
> And in the watches of the night they smart,
> But wounds like that are easily concealed,
> And who can tell what happens in the heart?
> They laid him in a tomb when day went down,
> And no-one knows what happened to the crown.

FIFTH LESSON

Leader: Hear the story of the passion of our Lord and of his trial before Pilate the governor.
(John 18:28–40 is read.)

The fifth candle is extinguished.

Congregational hymn:
When I Survey the Wondrous Cross

SIXTH LESSON

Leader: Hear the story of the passion of our Lord and of his scourging and condemnation.
(John 19:1–16 is read.)

The sixth candle is extinguished.

Choir/solo *O Come and Mourn with Me Awhile*

Poem *I am a squeamish person, Lord* by Margaret Knauerhase

I am a squeamish person, Lord.
I do not wish to see you die.
The whole affair is far too sad,
And I might cry.

I'd rather think of clothes or food
Or travel, or of anything.
I do not understand why God
Is suffering.

It's cruel what they do to you.
I'd like to get out, but the crowd
Is all around and shouting too –
It's all so loud!
Did I hear you implore, "Forgive,
They know not what they do"? Do I?
Lord, is it so that I may live
That you must die?

Why must I see? Why must I stay?
Your mother's there, and some few friends,
But I'll come back some other day
When all this ends.

So weak am I, and yet I feel
You have some strange, deep need of me.
How can I meet that mute appeal
I dare not see?

SEVENTH LESSON

Leader: Hear the story of the passion of our Lord and of his crucifixion on
Calvary.
(John 19:17–27 is read)

Audio visual

Slides of the agony of humanity (war, starvation, etc), set to quiet contemplative taped music

Choir/solo *Were You There When They Crucified My Lord?*

The seventh candle (still alight) is processed from the church.

The Lord's Prayer (spoken together – in darkness)

All: Our Father in heaven,
       hallowed be your name,
       your kingdom come,
       your will be done,
       on earth as in heaven.
       Give us today our daily bread.
       Forgive us our sins
       as we forgive those who sin against us.
       Save us from the time of trial
       and deliver us from evil.
       For the kingdom, the power, and the glory are yours
       now and forever. Amen.

Musical postlude:
    Quiet contemplative taped music is played as the congregation exits the
    church (which remains in darkness).

PROPHET AND PRIEST
A Passover re-enactment

Maundy Thursday

While the celebration of Passover continues to be a celebration of the Hebrew people, it is also special to Christians for its association with Holy Communion. The very powerful symbolism of Passover clearly lies behind Paul's theology of a sacrificial atonement, and it is, for us, a living testimony to God's saving grace, made personal in Jesus.

This service is not a communion service. It takes elements of Passover meals of the first century and recites the liturgy, as a means of entering into this part of the passion narrative. It helps us understand the setting in which Christ broke bread and shared the cup.

This is a teaching service. We come to understand Christ as the fulfilment of the law and the prophets. It is a teaching service through symbol and action, and parallels, in that sense, the cultic teaching of our ancestors in the faith.

If the service is conducted at the church property, it can be concluded by proceeding to any nearby grove (especially if an olive grove is possible), where the reading of Christ in the Garden of Gethsemane could be recited or re-enacted. A person kneeling at a distance by a lantern to resemble Christ will add to the effect.

If the service is conducted in homes, the various groupings could travel to the church and similarly process together to the grove. Using candles as the light source is particularly engaging for children, and creates a lovely atmosphere (not to mention witness on main roads!).

Introductory comments

The Jewish Passover is a thanksgiving festival in which the Hebrew people celebrate their deliverance from slavery in Egypt. God sent two messengers – Moses and Aaron – to beg Pharaoh to free the Hebrews. When he refused, ten plagues were sent to punish the Egyptians. The tenth and last plague was by far the worst. Through Moses, God threatened to kill the firstborn child and calf of every Egyptian family. Pharaoh refused to listen. After the tenth plague devastated the people, the Hebrews were freed. Eventually they came into the land God had promised them.

The Passover meal is a reminder of these events. The food is symbolic of the people's life in bondage and of God's salvation.

Unleavened bread (matzah) is used, since there was no time for the yeast to rise (yeast was also a symbol of impurity).
Wine is a symbol of God's goodness and the bounty of the Promised Land.

Parsley and celery stand for the hyssop which was used to smear lamb's blood on the Hebrews' doorposts, that the Lord might distinguish their households when he passed over the land.

Bitter herbs are a symbol of suffering.

Salt water is a symbol of the crossing of the Red Sea and of the Egyptians' tears.

Charoses is a symbol of the mortar and bricks the people were forced to make. (Charoses is a mixture of apple, nuts and cinnamon.)

Roast lamb was eaten in preparation for the Exodus.

Cup of Elijah: It was believed that this favourite prophet would come in spirit to share the meal.

Hallel: Psalms 113–118, psalms of praise to God, were sung during the meal.

The Great Hallel: Psalm 136 – this was most likely the psalm the disciples sang before going out to the Mount of Olives.

Participants:
> Host – usually the male head of the house.
> Hostess – usually the female head of the house.
> Child – young but able to read.
> Narrator – could be the host.
> Reader(s) – to read the passages of Scripture (could be the narrator).

The ritual conveys the truth that Israel's freedom is dependent upon God's sovereignty, power, and love.

For Christians, the meal has a different significance. Certainly, as the new Israel (or people of the new covenant), we inherit the same history. They are our ancestors. But the Passover is more personally significant in that the Holy Communion has its origin in our Lord's Last Supper, which was most likely a Passover meal. Jesus took these rich traditions and made them symbols of his life and death.

The Passover, a celebration of a nation's liberation, becomes, in the Christian rite, a celebration of salvation for all people.

PROPHET AND PRIEST

Welcome

Introduction

> Tonight we gather to celebrate the Passover, recalling the great traditions of our faith. We celebrate it as a family of God's people, recalling how Jesus once met with his disciples to share such a meal. In so doing, he made this meal a symbol of his own life, death, and resurrection. The risen Lord is present with his people. Let us join in fellowship around his table.

Song   *O God, Our Help in Ages Past* (based on Psalm 90)
> *(The hostess lights the candles during the hymn.)*

Opening prayer – Hostess

> Blessed are you, O King Eternal, our God, Ruler of the Universe. You have given us festival days for joy. Blessed are you who selected us from among all the people and exalted us among the nations and sanctified us with your commandments.

The first cup (The Cup of Blessing) is poured

Prayer of blessing – Host (*taking the cup*)

> Blessed are you, O God, you are Creator of the fruit of the vine. You have given us this feast of unleavened bread in remembrance of the time of our deliverance from bondage and of the departure from Egypt. Blessed are you, O Eternal One, for you hallow the festival days.

The Cup of Blessing is shared

Thanksgiving for the fruit of the earth – Host

> Let us take the appetizer of celery dipped in salt water. Remember how the Hebrews used hyssop to smear lamb's blood on their doorposts in Egypt on the night of the Passover.

> The salt water shall remind us of the Egyptians' tears and the water of the Red Sea through which our ancestors passed. Let us hear once again the story of these events.

Exodus 12:3–14 and Exodus 14:5–16, 21–23

All: Lord our God, let us always remember how you saved your people in Egypt. May we always understand that all people depend on your gracious blessing for salvation.
(A brief period of silent reflection follows.)

The breaking of unleavened bread

(The middle matzah is broken in two. One half is placed between the remaining two, the other hidden under a napkin next to the plate. The plate is lifted up, each person holding it as the prayer of the blessing of the bread is said.)

All: This is the bread of affliction which our ancestors ate in the land of Egypt. Let all who are hungry come and eat of it. Let all who have need come and share in the Passover's blessing.

The second cup is poured and shared

Song *From All Who Dwell Below the Skies* (based on Psalm 117)

The heritage

A young child: Why is this meal special? Why do we eat unleavened bread?

Host: Because our ancestors were slaves in Egypt and were brought forth by God's right hand. If God had not done this, we would still be slaves.

Young child: Why do we eat the bitter herbs and charoses?

Host: The bitter herbs remind us of our suffering, while the Charoses remind us of the mortar and bricks our ancestors were compelled to make.
Let us say grace together.

All: Blessed are you, O Lord, our God, who brings forth fruit from the earth. Blessed are you, O God, who has sanctified us with your commandment and enjoined us to eat unleavened bread.

The third cup is poured

The Passover meal – Host

> *(Each person shall receive two pieces of matzah. One is eaten with the bitter herbs, the other with the charoses. All the food must be eaten, for this is a meal recalling God's deliverance in bondage. All must be fully satisfied.)*

All: While our ancestors were in the wilderness for 40 years, God provided for them, and the food which he provided was sufficient for their needs. He led them into the land of Israel and took care of them. How much more are we indebted for the wonderful gifts of good things God has bestowed upon us.

(The meal is eaten.)

Host: Let the doors be opened that the Spirit of Elijah may enter. Let us bless God whose gifts we have eaten and through whose grace we have life.

All: Blessed be the name of the Lord forever.

Matthew 26:26–30

Song *An Upper Room Did Our Lord Prepare*

> *(The previously hidden piece of bread is broken and shared by all at the table. The cup of Elijah is taken and shared in like manner. In silence we think of the suffering of Christ and of our liberation through faith.)*

The Great Hallel

Song *Give to Our God Immortal Praise* (based on Psalm 136)

TABLE SETTING FOR PASSOVER

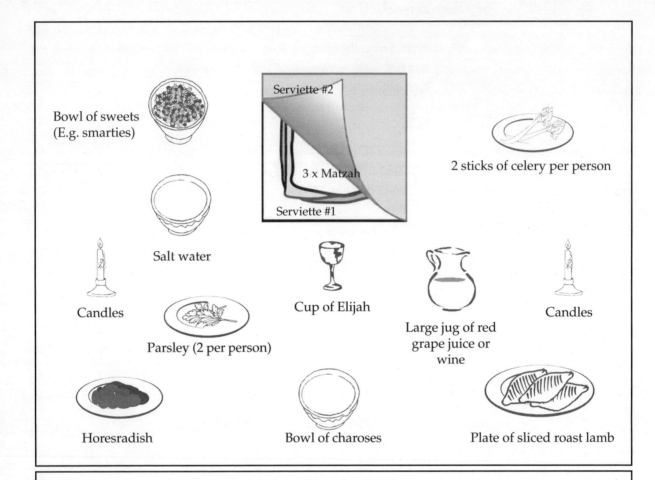

Bowl of sweets (E.g. smarties)

Serviette #2

3 x Matzah

Serviette #1

2 sticks of celery per person

Salt water

Candles

Parsley (2 per person)

Cup of Elijah

Large jug of red grape juice or wine

Candles

Horesradish

Bowl of charoses

Plate of sliced roast lamb

SETTING FOR EACH PARTICIPANT

Hymn Book

Red serviette

White plate or serviette

Glass or chalice

IT IS FINISHED
A Good Friday service

Good Friday is the most solemn and sacred day on the Christian calendar. It is hard for us to comprehend the full extent of its meaning. The atonement must always be more than we can grasp. The mystery of a God who enters our reality, accepting humiliation and rejection, ultimately dying for the forgiveness of our sins, will always be beyond our comprehension.

Good Friday is not a day for erudite theology or apologetics. There is something base about its brutality. It should horrify us. Even in an age of television violence, graphic depictions of war, and video games that invite the players to slaughter at will, this story is awful. It should touch us deep within, reviling us as we contemplate the killing of God's own self-revelation.

The event takes on archetypal significance, for in this event we find ourselves present. There is in us the battle between divine holiness and hostile sinfulness. We are invited to enter into the story, not just as onlookers, but also as participants. There are for us here crucial issues of life and death, goodness and evil, justice and selfishness.

This service seeks to do two things. First it tells the story through the "seven words" of Christ upon the cross. We listen to the pain and enter into this sacrificial act.

Second, it connects this act of the Christ with the pain and suffering of our world. Each of the words is connected with specific suffering.

The worship is repetitive. It is almost unbearable at times. People respond that they want to escape the darkness of it all. It becomes almost oppressive as it rolls through seven cycles of prayer and story. We are seeking to encounter the sense of shock and grief that accompanied this tragic event.

At the end, there is a call to respond. It is a call to identify with the suffering ones, and with the Christ who is found among them. The reaffirmation of baptism asks us to be one with the Suffering Servant in the work of redemption and healing.

Visuals
It is suggested that some time be given to thinking about the decorations and lighting. The lectern/pulpit, communion table, cross and font might all be draped in black cloth. A small flash of red cloth can be incorporated into the black of the cross.

A crown of thorns (large and imposing) should be placed on the communion table. Perhaps a closed Bible could lie on the floor in front of the communion table, to convey the sense that "the Word is crucified for us." (Of course, we live on the resurrection side of Easter, but it will help to offer symbols that allow participants to enter into the scandal of the event.)

Do not overdo the decorations with additional rugged crosses or spikes or whips. The crown is the primary focus. One could have the candelabra from the Tenebrae service somewhere in the background, or a chalice might lie on its side to depict the spilled blood of Christ, but essentially the thorns are our primary symbol. The feeling is one of starkness and hostility.

Minimal lighting in the church adds to the sense of gloom.

The thorns

Fashion a crown of thorns for the communion table (at least 35 cm. or 15 in. diameter). Cut up enough thorny spikes so that each worshipper will receive one during the worship. These will be given out as the service proceeds. You will need to take a rough count of the worshippers at the beginning of the service, divide by seven, and then give out that number each time as the song *Were You There* is sung. The sharper and longer the thorns are the better. People will use these for reflection as the service moves forward, and the fact that people do not all receive them at the same time adds its own dimensions. You may need two or three people for the distributing.

(Example: 100 worshippers = 7 lots of 14 thorns given out. At the end, ensure that **everyone** has a thorn twig.)

The reaffirmation of baptism

This is a most powerful liturgical act when associated with Good Friday. Invariably people protest that it should be offered only on Easter day, but those who have invited this response on Good Friday always attest to the power of this association.

In Mark 10:35–45, we read the encounter between Jesus and James and John. Here Jesus clearly links baptism, servanthood and suffering. In offering this reaffirmation on Good Friday, we are inviting disciples of Christ to identify with him as the Suffering Servant, and to be willing to identify with the suffering of the world.

When the people come forward, the minister/s will dip a finger in the font, name the person, and make the sign of the cross on their forehead saying,

"N, recall that the sign of the cross is upon you.
 Go, and live out your baptism."

If space permits, they may be invited to stay at the front to kneel in prayer, or stand beneath the cross or in front of the communion table. If not, instruct them to return to their seats, or if, as suggested, there is no conclusion to this service, invite them to sit and reflect until they are ready to leave. (Quiet, mournful, reflective music may be appropriate.)

Pastoral concerns

What about those people who are not baptized? Well, first it provides an interesting opportunity for raising the whole matter of the importance of baptism ahead of time. I have been offering this opportunity in worship on Good Friday for 15 years. It has provided an excellent opportunity for driving home that the rites and sacraments of the church have meanings.

It is, nonetheless, important to reinforce that everyone is welcome to come forward to make a response. A second place of prayer can be established for such people.

How do we know if a person is baptized or not? Again, this is a tricky question, but not one for splitting hairs over at the font. If the instructions are clear (it is best to make the point right at the beginning of the service that there will be a point of reaffirmation of baptism toward the end of the worship service), one may have to leave it to the integrity and nous of the individuals.

What about children? If children are a part of the normal liturgical life of a congregation, this is never a problem. Parents are used to helping their children make such responses. In fact, it can be overwhelming to see the sense of the sacred on the faces of children who have come forward. Over years of expecting children, youth, adults, and the elderly all to make a faith response in many different ways, a sense of the appropriateness of the invitation grows, as well as exercising grace rather than law in these circumstances.

Those who have not been baptized might come forward for prayer and a blessing without the reaffirmation of baptism.

One final word. It will be important to alert pastoral carers to keep an eye out for folk who may need counsel or prayer. This can be a time when many of the hurts of the past or uncertainties of faith and life emerge. Encourage the pastoral care team or elders to be aware of the need to get alongside anyone who is moved or distressed.

Music

For this particular service, the mood is one of heaviness. Dirges are appropriate, as is silence. Use music sparingly, perhaps more for covering movement noises than to direct the worship. The two songs are repeated, so that worshippers are able to move through the words to prayer. It may be necessary to learn the songs at the beginning. If other songs are chosen, use them repetitively rather than have a variety. It is the drudgery of solid liturgical work that is sustained by the repetition. Above all, don't let the congregation off the hook. They will thank you for drawing them more and more into the reality of Good Friday!

For this service, you will need:

- decorations
- crown of thorns
- enough thorns for one per worshipper
  (given out during the singing of *Were You There?*)
- liturgist
- people to read the "plights"
- font with water or bowls

The seven plights

In each section there is the identification of a particular group of sufferers. There is material provided for this focus, but identifying a very current issue or group, especially including some visuals, will be even more powerful. An interview with a refugee, or a statement by someone who has experienced the horrors of war or been in prison and so on, will make the service more personal. Use the resources of the congregation to bring the worship alive.

IT IS FINISHED

Crown of thorns
They have crowned you, Lord, with a crown of thorns.
They have gathered thorns from earth's cursed fields
And braided you a crown.

You receive the thorns,
You accept the strife and sorrow of this earth
And reshape it into a crown of victory.

To be aware is to suffer.
Your whole life is a willing suffering.
In your holy obedience, suffering is transformed
Into a king's shining crown.
Thus you prevail over suffering.

Out of earth's pain and sorrow
Must be brought forth strength and understanding.
You bring us healing from our sorrows.
In suffering you honour us with a crown.
Our pains are your gracious visitation.

You wear the crown of thorns.
You desire to draw us up – closer to you.
You desire to take us up – into victory.

Yes, Lord, I am ready.
Impress on me, thorn-crowned one, your image,
That I may become like you.

"Dornenkranz" by Karl Bernhard Ritter
Source unknown. Printed by *The Other Side,* Jan/Feb, 1983

Introduction
This intercessory service of worship is based upon a service developed by American Christians for the Abolition of Torture. In the introduction to the original, we read, "The service has been designed to assist faith communities relive the passion of Christ and remember that the sufferings of Christ continue through the plight of the poor, the oppressed, and the persecuted throughout the world."

At the end of the series of litanies, based upon the Seven Words of Christ, there will be a time of reflection during which recorded music will be played. There will be an opportunity for you to respond to the suffering Christ by making a reaffirmation of your baptism.

You are invited to leave the service when you feel it is appropriate. Hence the service will have no defined conclusion, but will look towards the celebration of the resurrection on Sunday.

In preparation of this act of worship, you are asked to reflect on the meditation "Crown of Thorns," on the previous page.

Dying, you destroyed our death
Dying, you destroyed our death,
Rising, you restored our life;
Lord Jesus, come in glory.
    (*three times*)

Words: Traditional
(Music for a sung version written by Rod Boucher is found in the songbook *All Together Again* (No. 171) Open Book Publishers, Adelaide)

WereYou There ?
Were you there when they crucified my Lord? *(Repeat)*
O sometimes, it causes me to tremble, tremble, tremble;
Were you there when they crucified my Lord?

Were you there when they nailed him to the tree? *(Repeat)*
O sometimes, it causes me to tremble, tremble, tremble;
Were you there when they nailed him to the tree?

Traditional Negro Spiritual

THE FIRST WORD

Leader: You wear the crown of thorns, Lord. It is a crown worn for those suffering because of their race.

People: We worship you, O Christ, and we praise you because in your suffering you redeem the world. Let us hear of the thorns which grow in earth's cursed fields and feel with those who share in your suffering.

Leader: Let us hear of the thorns…
People: That we might share in your suffering.

Song: *Dying, You Destroyed Our Death*

Scripture Father forgive...
Luke 23:32–34a

Leader: This is the word of the Lord.

People: Thanks be to God.

The plight of those experiencing racial persecution

Oh what a world this is!

The global village has become a killing field.

Empty-armed mothers cry for their baby corpses. Children roam aimlessly, desperately, looking for a familial face.

Fathers and sons are carted off, to be laid bloodied in an unmarked grave.

We have a name for it. We call it "ethnic cleansing," as though this antiseptic title will make it the more acceptable.

It is murder, fashioned by race and bigotry. Skin-deep hatred – a language that defines our worst and breeds terror in the hearts of all.

Who will it be?

Who will come with specified ideology for you and for me?

Our intercession

Leader: "We are a chosen race, a royal priesthood, a holy nation, God's own people, that we may declare the wonderful deeds of God who called us out of darkness into God's marvelous light." (1 Peter 2:9, paraphrase)

People: We remember the plight of the victims of racism. Hear our cry, O God. Break down the barriers in people's hearts that divide. Make us open to one another regardless of our differences. Help us to receive these thorns, so as to reshape the face of humanity.

Song *Were You There?*

(Silent prayer)

THE SECOND WORD

Leader: "When Jesus was made to suffer, he did not counter with threats, but delivered himself up to the One who judges justly."
(1 Peter 2:23)

People: We worship you, O Christ, and we praise you because in your suffering you redeem the world. Let us hear of the thorns which grow in earth's cursed fields and feel with those who share in your suffering.

Leader: Let us hear of the thorns...

People: That we might share in your suffering.

Song	*Dying, You Destroyed Our Death*
Scripture	Today you will be with me in paradise.
	Luke 23:39–43
Leader:	This is the word of the Lord.
People:	Thanks be to God.

The plight of those in overcrowded prisons and on death row

The Prison
Don't close the door.
Don't turn the key
on this poor cell today.
I am your flesh, can you not see
we are the same – yes, you and me.
Four walls – that is my destiny,
and here I'll stay or die.

I too have dreams,
a faith, and love.
I am not less for all my crimes.
There are those who grieve with me,
who share my shame, and pity me.
Four walls – not made of stone,
but mind and memory defined.

Remember me,
not for my crime,
lest common decency be lost,
for many fill such cells as mine,
and innocence their only crime.
Four walls – a prison cell to bind
a longing heart confined.

Our intercession

Leader:	Hear of the thorns that grow in earth's cursed fields. Be aware of those who wait for the state to decide their fate. You, too, O Christ, were imprisoned by righteous persons. Help us to have compassion in our judgment. Help us to receive these thorns. May they be reshaped into a crown of victory.

Song:	Were You There?
	(Silent prayer)

THE THIRD WORD

Leader: Out of earth's pain and sorrow must be brought forth strength and understanding. You bring us healing for our sorrows.

People: We worship you, O Christ, and we praise you because in your suffering you redeem the world. Let us hear of the thorns which grow in earth's cursed fields and feel with those who share in your suffering.

Leader: Let us hear of the thorns…

People: That we might share in your suffering.

Song: *Dying, You Destroyed Our Death*

Scripture: Woman, this is your son
(John 19:25b–27)

Leader: This is the word of the Lord.

People: Thanks be to God.

The plight of refugees

May 1999, and the Australian Navy boards a foreign vessel. Under surveillance as it journeyed up and down the eastern coastline, its captain sought a safe harbour to offload its cargo. Men, women and children, crammed in a container – a human cargo, escaping one last time, looking for a better home, for freedom and for life.

One face of the thousands who daily flee all they hold dear, forced from their homes by the greed of others, or some ideological imperative, or the impossible harshness of life. What drives them? A gun here, a storm there, a famine or a plague, perhaps their skin or religion does not fit. It matters little – all they know is they cannot stay, their very lives depend on their going!

"How many," you ask? The last census (July 1998) estimated more than 50 million – 22 million in foreign lands; 30 million displaced but still in their own lands.

Each one, just like you and me. They, too, have careers to pursue, or things to learn, or families to love. Their lives are just as precious as yours or mine. Now they bear the scars of knowing, as you and I can only imagine, just how fragile life and home and love can be.

Our intercessions

Leader: The Lord lifts up those who are bowed down; the Lord loves the righteous. The Lord watches over the sojourner; the Lord upholds the widow and the fatherless.
(Psalm 146:8–9, paraphrase)

People: Jesus Christ, your whole life was one of willing suffering. In your holy obedience, suffering is transformed into a shining crown. Thus you prevail over suffering. We remember the millions of refugees of this world. Help us receive these thorns, for to be aware is to suffer. Stir us to action for the sake of the powerless.

Song *Were You There?*

(Silent prayer)

THE FOURTH WORD

Leader: They have crowned you, Lord, with a crown of thorns,
They have gathered thorns from earth's cursed fields
and braided you a crown.

People: We worship you, O Christ, and we praise you because in your suffering you redeem the world. Let us hear of the thorns which grow in earth's cursed fields and feel with those who share in your suffering.

Leader: Let us hear of the thorns…

People: That we might share in your suffering.

Song: *Dying, You Destroyed Our Death*

Scripture: Eloi, Eloi, lama sabachthani!
(Matthew 27:45–46, NIV)

Leader: This is the word of the Lord.

People: Thanks be to God.

The plight of those suffering in war

So many guns, so many planes and bombs, so many rockets and grenades.
Tread carefully, friend, that step could be your last. Watch now, the marksman takes his aim.

It never ends, this senseless killing goes on and on and on.
Nations eye one another, defending an uneasy peace. One false move, and it'll all be on again.
War – what a hideous thing it is. A single decision that changes forever the lives of countless millions. A siren wails, and ants scurry for their holes before the first wave of bombers drop their lethal cargo. "Will my home be there when it is done?" "Will my bed be warm to comfort and ease the tiredness of the day?" "Will all I take for granted be robbed from me in one steely second?"

Will tomorrow come, or will this uncertain night be an eternal future?

Our intercessions

Leader: "When all the prisoners in a country are crushed and trampled under foot, when human rights are over-ridden in defiance of the Most High, when people are deprived of justice, does not the Lord see it?" (Lamentations 3:34–36)

People: In suffering, Jesus, you honor us with a crown. Our pains are your gracious visitation. We remember before you the suffering people of the world – especially our brothers and sisters in the… *(name particular concerns).* We remember those who long for justice. Help us to receive these thorns, to feel their pain, and to suffer with and for them.

Song *Were You There?*

(Silent prayer)

THE FIFTH WORD

Leader: "God fulfills the desire of all who fear God, and hears their cry, and saves them. God preserves all who love God, but will destroy all the wicked."
(Psalm 145:19–20, Inclusive Language Psalms)

People: We worship you, O Christ, and we praise you because in your suffering you redeem the world. Let us hear of the thorns which grow in earth's cursed fields and feel with those who share in your suffering.

Leader: Let us hear of the thorns…

People: That we might share in your suffering.

Song   *Dying, You Destroyed Our Death*

Scripture I thirst.
(John 19:28–29)

Leader:	This is the word of the Lord.
People:	Thanks be to God.

The plight of those suffering religious persecution

Our Father... Parent... Abba... Allah... What name do you prefer, God of a thousand names?

Call you by the wrong one and it will make all the difference – at least for me! Which do you really prefer, or does it not really matter to you?
I sometimes wonder whether you just hear **my** prayers, or whether you think each prayer is as good as another? Is there a right way to face or kneel or sit, or is the open heart enough for you?

We have a problem, God of a thousand names. We all think our way is the only way. We think your accent is the same as ours. Worst still, we think you are offended by anything else, offended enough for us to force our ways on all other ways. Isn't that what you want, God of a thousand names – to force, cajole, imprison or kill all who think another way? I'll do my best to show the error of all other ways. Then you'll be satisfied, and I will have the pleasure of knowing, I got it right.

What do you mean, you don't know me – I'm one of yours!

Our intercessions

Leader:	Jesus said, "If the world hates you, know that it has hated me before it hated you... If they persecuted me, they will persecute you." *(John 15:18, 20, RSV)*
People:	As you had courage to suffer death, give us the courage to live in faithful witness to you. Let us remember those who are being persecuted for their religious beliefs. Let us remember those who defend freedom of conscience. We especially pray for the people of (name particular places where religious persecution is felt).
	Help us to receive these thorns, for thus can we suffer with our own.

Song: *Were You There?*

(Silent prayer)

THE SIXTH WORD

Leader: Feel their pain, hear their cry: let them touch you deep in your heart. Christ died to heal and save the exploited. Blessed be the name of the Lord.

People: We worship you, O Christ, and we praise you because in your suffering you redeem the world. Let us hear of the thorns which grow in earth's cursed fields and feel with those who share in your suffering.

Leader: Let us hear of the thorns…

People: That we might share in your suffering.

Song *Dying, You Destroyed Our Death*

Scripture It is finished.
(John 19:30)

Leader: This is the word of the Lord.

People: Thanks be to God.

The plight of exploited workers

New shoes! The best on the market – and what a bargain. You won't believe what I can get these for in Indonesia. Not quite as cheap as Vietnam, but then the hotels aren't as plush up there.

It all has to do with trade – or something. The people love to work up there. They'll do it for practically nothing. And they're so easy going. You'd think with such cheap prices they'd all be wearing designer labels, but no, they prefer their traditional ways. Strange, eh?

I think it's why they look so unhappy. I can't fathom it – all that gear, cheap prices, and tons of work. I tell you, it's paradise.

I wouldn't want to live there though.

Our intercessions

Leader: The enemy pursues my soul; he has crushed my life to the ground: he has made me dwell in darkness like the dead, long forgotten. Therefore my spirit fails; my heart is numb within me.

People: O God, we remember the powerless peasants of the land; the children forced to work for a pittance; those exploited in the work forces of the world. Lord, you accepted the strife and sorrow of this world. Reshape it into a crown of justice.

Song   *Were You There?*

(Silent prayer)

THE SEVENTH WORD

Leader: They came for Jesus in the dead of night. They took him away to be tortured and to die. We turn to pray for those who are made to "disappear" because they have been found "inconvenient" by someone in power.

People: We worship you, O Christ, and we praise you because in your suffering you redeem the world. Let us hear of the thorns which grow in earth's cursed fields and feel with those who share in your suffering.

Leader: Let us hear of the thorns…

People: That we might share in your suffering.

Song: *Dying, You Destroyed Our Death*

Scripture: Father, into your hands…
(Luke 23:44–46)

Leader: This is the word of the Lord.

People: Thanks be to God.

The plight of the disappeared

An empty chair, a silent voice, a vivid memory growing dimmer with the years.

Some deaths you can make sense of – but when someone just disappears, how do you make sense of that? How do you say your goodbyes? How do you stop longing for them to turn a corner, or open a door, or hold you in their arms again?

A rare occurrence?

In our lifetimes the number of disappearances is staggering: 15,000 Argentines; 100,000 Ugandans; 9,000 in the Kabul region of Afghanistan; and how many in Bosnia, or Kosova?

These people have not vanished. Someone planned their abduction. Someone is responsible for their terror, their torture, their lonely deaths.
Often in the dead of night, a knock on the door and…

Our intercessions

Leader: Let your heart be pierced by this thorn. Sense the agony of unknowing. Feel the terror of waiting.

People: We remember the disappeared. We remember their loved ones. Thank you, Mother of all life, that you were present and that you received them. In faith we pray for eternal life. In hope, we pray for mercy. Help us to receive these thorns. May they be reshaped into a crown of victory.

Song: *Were You There?*

(Silent prayer)

CONCLUDING PRAYERS

Leader: Many are the cursed fields of the earth. All humanity cries out in lament. Let us pray with one mind and one heart with the crucified body of Christ.

All: Out of the depths I cry to you, O Lord. Lord, hear my voice! Let your ears be attentive to the voice of my supplications.

If you, O Lord, mark our iniquities, Lord, who can stand? But there is forgiveness with you, so that you may be revered.

I wait for the Lord, my soul waits and in his word I hope;
my soul waits for the Lord, more than those who watch for the morning, more than those who watch for the morning.
O Israel, hope in the Lord!

For with the Lord there is steadfast love,
and with [God] is great power to redeem.
It is [God] who will redeem Israel for all its iniquities.
   (Psalm 130)

(Silent meditation)

During this time, you are invited to come to the baptismal font to reaffirm your commitment to stand with the suffering Christ in our suffering world. There you will be reminded that, at your baptism, you received the blessing and challenge of Christ's cross.

A minister will mark your forehead with water in the sign of the cross and say, "Recall that the sign of the cross is upon you. Go, and live out your own baptism." If you wish to take this opportunity to reaffirm your commitment to our Lord, come reverently when you have prepared yourself in this time of prayer. You may prefer to simply come to the front for a blessing.

As Jesus' death is incomplete without his resurrection, this service has no conclusion until Easter Sunday. When you are ready, you are asked to retire from the worship center.

CHRIST IS RISEN!
Easter Day service

Introduction
The Easter celebration is the natural conclusion to the Good Friday service. All the doom and gloom is suddenly transformed into joy and wonder. For contemporary Christians, this is a wonderful celebration, but the surprise and mystery can be a little taken for granted.

To experience the transforming power of the resurrection, one might begin exactly where we left off on Friday. The church is without lights. All the black cloth is still in place. The misery and gloom of the tomb is still present. The prelude is a dirge.

The call to worship heralds another dimension. Perhaps the minister or leader of worship is moving to the lectern to begin, but young women run through the sanctuary shouting "He is alive," a trumpet fanfare follows, and the choir or leader of worship cries out with hands raised in jubilation, "Christ is risen!" Or perhaps it begins with a murmur in the choir, and a few in the congregation begin to repeat, softly at first, then growing louder and louder, "Christ is risen," until the worship leader leaps to her or his feet and exclaims "Christ is risen!"

Then, as the processional hymn is sung, the lights are turned on, the black is dramatically removed, and flowers, balloons, streamers waved by children, the Bible, Christ candle, and communion elements are ushered in. Before the congregation's eyes Easter transforms the very setting in which they are worshipping. One could have children dressed as clowns dancing down the aisles to lead the procession.

The atmosphere
Easter Sunday has the feel of joy-filled urgency. One has the sense of the women running to tell the others; or the two on the road hastening back to Jerusalem to share their experience.

Throughout, the liturgists have to work hard to maintain the sense of joy and excitement. In a sense, the climax of the service comes with the call to worship. We do not come down from it, however. We maintain the infectious happiness as much as possible.

In the children's focus time, they might be invited to hand out small Easter eggs to everyone in the congregation. The story of *Philip's Easter Egg* lends itself to this.

Our God is a lavish and generous being, who withholds nothing from us. This is a day for the flowers to be stunning, the music bright and full of pace, and all to be wearing smiles.

In some churches, hot cross buns are served after the worship. If there is a way to get the smell of them warming to move through the congregation toward the end of worship, this will provide more expectation for the senses.

The Communion
One way of getting across the power of the cross and the risen Christ is to have the communion bread baked in the shape of the cross. To have it processed in held aloft can make a great impact. The same with the wine. To have five, six, or seven people carrying in the glasses, or holding aloft one, two, three, or four chalices conveys the abundance of God's grace.

Perhaps, this Sunday, the communion could be received in the pews, with enough servers to serve just three rows each so that it is done very quickly. Perhaps the elements will be received together as a sign that we all are sharers in the joy of the occasion.

For this service, you will need:
- liturgists
- preacher
- readers
- musicians
- singers
- decorations
- processional
- Holy Communion
- Easter eggs (optional)
- floral decorations

CHRIST IS RISEN!

Prelude

Call to worship

Trumpet fanfare

Leader: Christ is risen!
People: Christ is risen indeed!

Processional hymn
> *Christ the Lord Is Risen Today*

Prayer of adoration and praise
> All glory and honor, praise and adoration be given to you, almighty God. You have defeated, forever, the power of death, inviting all your children to enter into the wonder of Christ's resurrection. You unite us in a common humanity, declaring that there are no barriers to communion with you. You break down all the walls that divide, and invite us to share in the joy of salvation.
>
> We praise you for your loving kindness. We thank you that you lead us out of darkness into the wonder of your divine glory. You redeem our humanity, affirming us and loving us all.
>
> Lord Jesus Christ, gift of eternal life, thank you for enduring the pain of the cross that our sin might be forgiven. Thank you for making us sharers in the resurrection. May we always praise your name and honour you by our faithfulness.
>
> Holy Spirit, promise of eternal life, we rejoice in your presence, and pray that you might move among us here, to reshape us into the very likeness of the Christ. Make us a body, worthy of Jesus. Help us to be Christ to our world.
>
> In all things, O God, may we be one with you. May we delight you in worship, and be a blessing to others. For the sake of Jesus Christ, our redeemer, we pray. Amen.

Psalm 118:14–22 (a paraphrase)

Leader: The Lord is our strength and the joy of our hearts,
People: and has become our salvation.

Leader: There is a sound of triumphant praise
People: rising from God's faithful people.

Leader:	The power of God has been displayed!
People:	All can see that there is no limit to the Spirit's awesome might!
Leader:	We have inherited the gift of eternal life,
People:	and will declare the wonderful deeds of the Lord.
Leader:	We have been rebuked,
People:	but God did not hand us over to death.
Leader:	Open then the gates of righteousness;
People:	we will enter them; we will celebrate the goodness of God with thanksgiving.
Leader:	This is the way that the Lord has opened;
People:	let the faithful enter into the Lord's glory.
Leader:	We will give thanks to you, our Savior
People:	for you make us whole.
Leader:	The very stone which the builders rejected
People:	has become the chief cornerstone.
Leader:	This is the Lord's doing,
People:	and it is marvelous in our eyes.
Leader:	On this day the Lord has acted;
People:	we will rejoice and be glad in it.
Leader:	Hosanna, Lord, hosanna!
People:	Hosanna, Lord, hosanna!

Kids of all ages *Philip's Easter Egg*

> *(Children may be invited to give out small Easter eggs.)*

Anthem or singing group

Scripture   Matthew 28:1–10

Song   *Hail, Thou Once Despised Jesus*

Address

Song   *And Can It Be*

Notices and offering

> Offertory Prayer
>
> Almighty God, by your power you have changed life forever. There is no limit to what you can do. We dedicate this offering and our lives in your service. May we be bearers of eternal life. May all we

do and all we have be used to bring new life to our world. May we be an offering of grace in your name. Amen.

Prayers for others

Leader: Let us recall that Christ died for the sake of all. Let us remember that in his resurrection, God declares that all may know Christ's love and grace. So let us come to pray for all who are in need, that they may be enveloped in his saving power.

We pray for those known to us who are broken in body, mind or spirit.

People: O Spirit of the risen Christ, bring healing. (*Silent prayer*)

Leader: We pray for people who have lost their way.
People: O Spirit of the risen Christ, bring hope. (*Silent prayer*)

Leader: We pray for those who find it hard to believe.
People: O Spirit of the risen Christ, bring faith. (*Silent prayer*)

Leader: We pray for those who suffer the ravages of war, oppression and injustice.
People: O Spirit of the risen Christ, give courage and strength to endure. (*Silent prayer*)

Leader: Lord Jesus Christ, we thank you that you enter the reality of our lives and minister to our needs by your grace.
People: May we always be aware of the blessing of your Spirit forever at work in the world. Amen.

HOLY COMMUNION

The Peace
Leader: The peace of the Lord be always with you.
People: And also with you.

Great prayer of thanksgiving
Leader: The Lord be with you.
People: And also with you.

Leader: Lift up your hearts.
People: We lift them to the Lord.

Leader: Let us give thanks to the Lord our God.
People: It is right to give our thanks and praise.

Leader: How can we stop from praising you, for your mercy and love are beyond our comprehension. In the beginning, you created a beautiful universe where all things had their place and order. You infused it with your Spirit, and breathed life into all creatures. You made humankind in your own image, and though we often stray from you, you continually call us out of darkness into your light.

You call us to yourself, giving us leaders, prophets, priests and kings to create a holy nation. At the right time, you entered into our reality with the gift of Jesus, and have opened forever the doors to eternal life.

Now, in the age of the Spirit, you pour out your blessing on all, and make us your very own body. We thank you, and pray that we may be one with you now through this sacred meal. Let this bread be for us the food of eternal life. Let this cup be our nourishment, for we would take in your very grace, by which we are healed and made whole.

The breaking of the bread

Leader: Recall that on the night in which he was betrayed, our Lord took bread, and when he had given thanks, he broke it, and gave it to the disciples saying, "This is my body, given for you. Eat this in remembrance of me."

Then after the supper, again giving thanks, he took the cup saying, "Drink of this all of you. This is my blood of the new covenant which is shed for you and for many for the forgiveness of sins. Do this as often as you drink it, in remembrance of me."

Leader: (breaking the bread) This is the food of eternal life.
Jesus, Lamb of God,

People: have mercy on us.

Leader: *(raising the cup)* This is the cup of the new covenant.
Jesus, bearer of our sins,

People: have mercy on us.

Leader: These are the gifts of God for the people of God.
Jesus, redeemer of the world,

People: grant us peace.

THE COMMUNION

Prayer after Communion

By your grace you have fed us.
By your love you have nurtured us.
By your Word you have taught us,
and by your Spirit you have empowered us.
Lead us now from here, to be your faithful disciples,
for the sake of Christ, and in whose name we pray,

The Lord's Prayer

All: Our Father in heaven,
hallowed be your name,
your kingdom come,
your will be done,
on earth as in heaven.
Give us today our daily bread.
Forgive us our sins
as we forgive those who sin against us.
Save us from the time of trial
and deliver us from evil.
For the kingdom, the power, and the glory are yours
now and forever. Amen.

Song   *I Know That My Redeemer Lives*

Benediction

The Lord bless you and keep you;
The Lord make his face to shine upon you,
and be gracious unto you;
the Lord lift up his countenance upon you,
and give you peace.
(The Aaronic Blessing, Numbers 6:24–26)

May the love of God,
the grace of Christ,
and the resurrection power of the Spirit,
be with us forevermore.

All: Amen.

Postlude

Philip's Easter Egg

There was a young boy named Philip, who was born with Down's Syndrome, which means his mind didn't grow at the same rate as his body. He was happy, but he knew that he wasn't the same as other children. Philip went to Sunday school every Sunday, and was in a class with nine other eight-year-old boys and girls. Sometimes people aren't very friendly to someone different from themselves. That's how it was with Philip. The teacher carefully included Philip in all the activities, and the children tried very hard, but Philip was not really a part of that group. Philip, of course, did not choose or want to be different; he just was.

At Easter, the teacher had a great idea for a lesson. The teacher had collected 12 plastic containers that look like big eggs, to use that Sunday. Each child was given one. It was a beautiful day, and the task was to go outside on the church grounds and find a symbol for new life, put it into the plastic egg, and bring it back to the classroom. They would then open and share their new life symbols one by one. They did this and it was glorious. And it was confusing. And it was wild. They ran all around, gathered their symbols, and returned to the classroom.

They put the big eggs on a table and the teacher opened them. In the first one, there was a flower, and the children ooed and aahed. He opened another, and there was a little bud. He opened another and there was a rock. Some children laughed, and some said, "That's crazy. How's a rock supposed to be like new life?" But the girl whose egg it was spoke up. She said, "I knew all of you would get flowers, and buds, and leaves, and butterflies, and things like that. So I got a rock because I wanted to be different, and for me that's new life." The teacher went on opening the eggs.

He opened the last one, and there was nothing in it. Some children said, "That's silly. Somebody didn't do it right." The teacher felt a tug on his shirt and looked down. Philip was standing beside him. "It's mine," Philip said. "It's mine." And the children said, "You don't ever do things right, Philip. There's nothing there!" "I did so do it," Philip said. "I did do it. It's empty. The tomb is empty." There was silence. Then Jason said, "What a terrific idea." The rest of the children joined in. "Philip had the best surprise." From that time on, Philip became a real part of that group. The whole class discovered new life because they had discovered that every person has something special to give. It didn't matter any more that Philip was different. They all knew he belonged there.

Philip died the next summer. His family had known since the time that he was born that he wouldn't live out a full life-span. Many other things had been wrong with his tiny body. On that day at the funeral nine eight-year-old children paraded right up to the altar, not with flowers, but with an empty plastic egg. They placed it on the altar in celebration of Philip's new life.

From *The Whole People of God*,
Used by permission of Wood Lake Books Inc.

Chapter six

O' Taste and See that the Lord is Good

Pentecost

This is a very different style of worship for Pentecost. In Acts 2:43–47, we have an interesting glimpse into the corporate life of the early church. One part of this is described as "they broke bread at home and ate their food with glad and generous hearts." Many commentators hold that this is the early origin of the Eucharist or Holy Communion. The first churches gathered and worshipped in homes, especially in places where there was persecution.

The Agape meal was a part of the first gatherings of Christians. It was an actual meal, not a stylized communion service with only bread and wine. It had its origins in the family meal, the feast days of the Hebrew people, and specifically the Passover meal.

While it may be disputed that this was Holy Communion, there is no doubt that the house church with fellowship around the table was a special part of the hospitality and worship of the early church.

A feature of the community after Pentecost was its openness, care for one another, and the exercising of the gifts of the Spirit.

This service could be held at the church, but it will be especially helpful in homes. A special night could be set aside for gatherings in homes around the congregation. Participants are invited to bring a dish for the meal. It should be their best meal, presented in their best china. The more succulent, the more delicious, the better. This is a celebration of the lavish provision of God, whose Spirit is poured out on us all.

The work of the Holy Spirit is to break down barriers, unite us in fellowship, empower the community of faith for service, and seal us as God's own children. These will be the marks of our gathering together. The spirit of the gathering will be celebratory, a sense of thanksgiving for the goodness of God.

Provisions
The host needs to provide a large loaf of bread and jugs of wine and/or unfermented grape juice as the beverage. The host will also need to set the table as for a feast or dinner party, including candles for lighting.

In this liturgy the **Host** will lead the liturgical prayers, and the **Leader** will lead reflections and discussions.

AN AGAPE MEAL

Host: O taste and see that the Lord is good.

All: God's love endures forever.

Host: Praised are you, living God, the eternal one, who has sanctified our lives through your commandments, commanding us to kindlethe festival lights.
The candles are lit

The Grace

Host: Blessed are you, O Lord our God, for giving us life, sustaining us and enabling us to celebrate your goodness.

The bread is raised

Host: Blessed are you, gracious and loving God, who brings forth bread for us to eat.

All: The work of human hands, and the fruit of the earth.

The wine/juice is raised

Host: Blessed are you, gracious and generous God, you bring forth fruit for us to share.

All: The work of human hands, and the fruit of the vine.

Host: O taste and see that the Lord is good.

All: God's love endures forever.

(The meal is begun. The bread is broken in large "chunks" – one for each person. The wine/juice is poured.)

Host: Jesus said, "I am the bread of life. Whoever comes to me will never be hungry."

All: We praise the name of the Lord.

Host: Jesus said, "I am the true vine." "Whoever believes in me will never be thirsty."

All: We praise the name of the Lord.
The meal is eaten.

During the meal, participants are invited to reflect on the gifts and ministry that they have received from the Holy Spirit. At the conclusion of the liturgy, you will find materials for the discussion.

At the conclusion of the meal, the host leads in thanksgiving.

Host: May the One whose food we have eaten be praised, now and forever.

All: Praised be our God, of whose bounty we have partaken and by whose grace we live.

Leader: Let us live in peace with each other and all living creatures.

All: Now and forevermore. Amen.

God's gifts for us all

Introduction:
Have you every stopped to evaluate the gifts Christ has given you? The Scripture passages below indicate some of the gifts he makes available through the Holy Spirit. Read the scriptures through, then tick the response that best describes your relationship to each of the gifts of the Spirit.

Readings   Ephesians 4:4–12
              1 Corinthians 12:8–10

	NOT ME	I DON'T THINK SO	NO IDEA	COULD BE	HONESTLY YES
PREACHING: I seem able to find the right words to communicate God's Word to others.					
SERVING: I find great delight in being available to other people. I like to help, and even simple tasks give me satisfaction.					
TEACHING: I have an ability to convey aspects of the Christian faith in such a way that others find easy to understand.					
ENCOURAGING: I sense an inner confidence and enthusiasm that helps others to face difficulties and challenges with courage.					
SHARING: I am aware that all I have is God's and am willing to make my resources available to those who need them.					
LEADING: People take note of what I say and do. They often look to me before making decisions.					
HELPING: I am happy to support the efforts of my Christian brothers and sisters, being available in whatever way I can.					

	NOT ME	I DON'T THINK SO	NO IDEA	COULD BE	HONESTLY YES

WISDOM: I seem able to identify the consequences of decisions. Sometimes I draw on experience; other times I am aware of what is the "best" path to follow.

KNOWLEDGE: I often have insight into the way that God wants us to be and act in a particular situation.

FAITH: In time of distress I know an inner assurance that helps me and others to stand firm.

HEALING: I have an inner capacity that allows me to be a channel for God's reconciliation that results in wholeness.

MIRACLES: There are times when God works through us in totally unexpected and unusual ways to affect God's will.

PROPHECY: I feel an inner compulsion to speak God's message to those God wants to address.

DISCERNMENT: I am able to distinguish between actions and ideas that really come from God and are according to God's will, and those that are not.

TONGUES: I find particular joy in praising God with my whole being that results in the uttering of strange sounds.

INTERPRETATION: I am able to say what God is saying through another speaking in tongues.

What is your role in the body of Christ?

The Apostle Paul not only provides us with an insight into some of the personal gifts of the Holy Spirit, but also indicated five ministries that make each Christian an essential gift to the body. *(Ephesians 4:4–12).*

Below are lists of gifts that could be considered part of the makeup of each ministry. In order to discover the gift that God is making you to be in the body, check the personal gifts you have already identified in the list. Which ministry do most of your gifts come under?

For example, if you identified preaching, leading, faith, and tongues, you may be an Apostle.

If you find it hard to identify your ministry, stop and pray that the Spirit will reveal it to you now.

These categories might help.

APOSTLE	PROPHET	EVANGELIST	PASTOR	TEACHER
Preaching	Preaching	Preaching	Serving	Teaching
Serving	Leading	Teaching	Encouraging	Encouraging
Encouraging	Wisdom	Encouraging	Sharing	Sharing
Leading	Knowledge	Faith	Helping	Leading
Wisdom	Prophecy	Healing	Healing	Knowledge
Knowledge	Tongues	Miracles	Discernment	Discernment
Faith	Interpretation	Prophecy	Tongues	Interpretation

APPENDIX

Considering the music

Where possible, we have chosen songs from well-known hymn books. Christmas carols can be found in many places. Most of the songs will be found in the four Openbook songbooks in the *All Together* series.

Where we think the source may be difficult to find, we have indicated possibilities below. It needs to be stressed that the music and poetry is offered as a suggestion only, and most congregations will have suitable music that is better chosen to suit their own community.

Abbreviations: TIS   *Together in Song 1999* (HarperCollins *Religious*)
                   SA   *Sing Alleluia 1987* (Collins)

Chapter two

Hymns: *Come, Thou Long Expected Jesus*
            O come, O come, Emmanuel

Other: *Light One Candle* Words and music by Natalie Sleeth,
              from *All God's Children Sing*, No. 13 (Wood Lake Books)

            Christ Be Our Light Words and music by Bernadette Farrell,
              from *All Together OK*, No. 313 (Openbook Publishers)

Chapter three

Hymns: *Away in a Manger*
            Hark the Herald Angels Sing
            Infant Holy, Infant Lowly
            Joy to the World
            Love Came Down at Christmas
            O Come, All Ye Faithful
            O Little Town of Bethlehem
            Once in Royal David's City
            Silent Night
            The First Nowell
            While Shepherds Watched

Other: *A Christmas Blessing* Words by Aubrey Podlich, music by Robin Mann,
              from *All Together Again*, No. 194 (Openbook Publishers)

            And He Shall Feed His Flock by Handel from *The Messiah*

            Angels We Have Heard on High by John Ness Beck

            Christmas Carols and Codas. Arr. John Ness Neck

            Benedictus by Darros, Published by Casa Musicale & Co. Milan

Cloth for the Cradle Words and arrangement by John L. Bell and Graham Maule from *Heaven Shall Not Wait* (W. G. R. G. Pearce Institute, Glasgow)

Donkey, Donkey Words and music by Leigh Newton, from *GOD Gives…Songs for Kids Book 2 (JBCE)*

O Christmas Tree Traditional, arranged by Norman Lloyd, from *Christmas Carols*, selected and arranged by Karle Sculte (Golden Press)

O Come Adore Him by Franz Schubert, from *Classic Canons*, Alfred Publishing Co. English words by Patrick M. Lieberge

Once You Had Silver Lyrics by Roma Ryan, music composed by Enya and Rick Ryan, from *The Memory of Trees* (Panda Press)

The Magnificat (choose a version such as *Tell Out My Soul*)

Turning Point of Time Words by Neil Quintrell, music by Douglas Simper, from *Songs for the Still Strange Land (JBCE)*

We Three Kings by John H Hopkins, from *Christmas Carols*, selected and arranged by Karle Sculte (Golden Press)

Chapter four

Hymns:			
	Have Faith in God, My Heart		
	Here I Am, Lord	TIS	658
	The Power of Your Love	TIS	685
	Jesus, You Have Come to the Lakeshore		
	O God, Our Help		
	The Great Love of God		

Other:			
	Comfort, Comfort	SA	25
	Father Welcomes	SA	34
	In the House of God by Robin Mann, from *All Together Now*, No. 10 (Openbook Publishers)		
	Prayer of St. Francis	SA	66

Spirit of Peace Words by D. A. Simper, music by L. N. Quintrell, from *All Together Again*, No. 192 (Openbook Publishers)

Chapter five

Hymns:	
	And Can It Be
	An Upper Room Did Our Lord Prepare
	Christ the Lord is Risen Today
	From All Who Dwell Below the Skies
	Give to Our God Immortal Praise
	Hail, Thou Once Despised Jesus
	I Know That My Redeemer Lives
	O Come and Mourn With Me Awhile

O Sacred Head, Sore Wounded
O God, Our Help in Ages Past
Were You There…
When I Survey the Wondrous Cross
When my love to Christ grows weak

Other: *Bitter Was the Night* by Sydney Carter,
from *All Together Again*, No. 135 (Openbook Publishers)
Dying you destroyed our death Words traditional, music for a sung version
written by Rod Boucher is found in the songbook *All Together Again*, No. 171
(Openbook Publishers)

O Lord, hear my prayer by Jaques Berthier, as published in *All Together Everybody*, No.
282 (Openbook Publishers)
also in *Together in Song*, No. 741 (HarperCollins *Religious*)

Footnotes

[1] T. S. Elliot, "Burnt Norton" from *Four Quartets* (New York: Harcourt Brace & Co., 1943, 1971), pp. 15, 16

[2] Invite a young woman dressed as Mary to sing a version of the Magnificat.

[3] Luke 1:19 (NRSV)

[4] Jon Walton, *Home for Christmas, Pulpit Digest* Nov/Dec 1998, page 78

[5] A. A. Milne, *Winnie the Pooh, The House at Pooh Corner* (London: Methuen Children's Books, London, 1995), p. 209

[6] Carlo Carretto et. al., *The God Who Comes* (New York: Orbis Books, 1974), p. 93.

[7] JAK 1995

Other resources from Wood Lake Books and Northstone you will find useful:

Living the Christ Life
Rediscovering the Seasons of the Christian Year
LOUISE MANGAN AND NANCY WYSE WITH LORI FARR
A valuable program resource offering activities, crafts, prayers, meditations and more.
Follows the cycles of Christmas and Easter.
ISBN 1-55145-498-X

Youth Spirit
Program Ideas for Youth Groups
COMPILED BY CHERYL PERRY
Games, reflection questions, worship suggestions and explanations of the church year.
ISBN 1-55145-247-2

Youth Spirit 2
Program Ideas for Youth Groups
ISBN 1-55145-500-5

Live the Story
Short Simple Plays for Church Groups
COMPILED BY CHERYL PERRY
Plays cover every major church celebration and are suitable for all ages and skill levels.
Cross-referenced by biblical passage, topic and season.
ISBN 1-55145-245-6

Learning Module boxed sets include everything needed for a complete program: Vacation Bible School, midweek groups, retreats, church camps, or a section within an existing program.

A People on the Move
Moses, Miriam, Aaron and the Exodus of the Hebrew People
MARILYN PERRY
Takes an exciting journey through the book of Exodus.
ISBN 1-55145-391-6

The Story of the Bible
How the World's Bestselling Book Came to Be
CHERYL PERRY
Learn about the Bible through fun, innovative activities. Also suitable for confirmation classes.
ISBN 1-55145-298-7

Family Ties
The Adventures of Abraham & Sarah & Their Descendants
ALYSON HUNTLY
Based on Genesis 12-50. Includes a video.
ISBN 1-55145-344-4

Easter Stories
The Family Story Bible Curriculum Module 2
JULIE ELLIOT
Share the stories of Easter with children aged 3-10. Includes Planning Guide with six lesson plans and a video of the stories.
ISBN 1-55145-434-3

The Birth & Childhood Stories of Jesus
The Family Story Bible Curriculum Module 1
PEGGY EVANS
Share these stories with young children anytime – at Vacation Bible School, and during midweek programs. Includes Planning Guide with six lesson plans and a video of the stories.
ISBN 1-55145-390-8

Marriage and Baptism Resources

When A Couple Marries
Couple's Pak Protestant   0-929032-61-6
Leader' Guide Protestant 0-929032-24-1

Couple's Kit   Catholic 532-6944
Leader's Guide Catholic 2-89088-463-5

Our Baby's Being Baptized
MARILYN PERRY
The events of Baptism for children 2 to 8 years.
ISBN 0-929-032-70-5

Your Child's Baptism
Wood Lake Books/Novalis
The tradition and theology of Baptism.
ISBN 1-55145-074-7 Protestant

My Baptism
BEV MILTON
Space to write the child's baptism next to Jesus' baptism. Full colour artwork, documents envelope, space for photos and family tree. Gift boxed.
1-55145-296-0 Hardcover

Titles for Group Study

John for Beginners
A Bible Study for Individual & Group Use
JAMES TAYLOR
This Bible study opens up new avenues of thought. Based on the Revised Common Lectionary. Includes questions and prayers.
ISBN 1-55145-496-3

The Spirit of Life
Five Studies to Bring Us Closer to the Heart of God
IAN PRICE
Guides readers through a five-session group study of selected scripture passages.
ISBN 1-55145-432-7

A Sensual Faith
Experiencing God Through Our Senses
IAN PRICE
This five-session group study explores each of the five senses as a doorway to deepening our faith and encountering God.
ISBN 1-55145-502-1

Jacob's Blessing
Dreams, Hopes and Visions for the Church
DONNA SINCLAIR & CHRISTOPHER WHITE
A hopeful and inspirational vision of the future of the church. Video and study guide also available.
ISBN Book: 1-55145-381-9   ISBN Video: 1-55145-388-6

Titles from Northstone Publishing that stimulate discussion

Religious Abuse
KEITH WRIGHT

This positive book opens the door to discussion of an issue that affects millions of churchgoers.
ISBN 1-896836-47-X

Prayer
The Hidden Fire
TOM HARPUR

Brings the broad theological perspective of prayer to the personal level.
ISBN 1-896836-40-2

Spiritscapes
Mapping the Spiritual and Scientific Terrain at the Dawn of the New Millennium
MARK PARENT

An overview and analysis of nine of the most significant spiritual and scientific movements of our time.
ISBN 1-896836-11-9

Secret Affairs of the Soul
Ordinary People's Extraordinary Experiences of the Sacred
PAUL HAWKER

Firsthand accounts of spiritual experiences from a broad range of individuals.
ISBN 1-896836-42-9

WOOD LAKE BOOKS NORTHSTONE

Northstone is an imprint of Wood Lake Books Inc.

Find these titles at any fine bookstore, or call 1.800.663.2775 for more information.
Check our website www.joinhands.com